D0913422

NO ONE HAS EVER DROWNED IN SWEAT

I AM STRONGER THAN THIS CHALLENGE.

NO ONE HAS EVER DROWNED IN SWEAT

HOPE IS SOMEWHERE BETWEEN TAKE OFF AND LANDING.

WHEN SOMETHING BAD HAPPENS YOU HAVE THREE CHOICES. YOU CAN LET IT DEFINE YOU, LET IT DESTROY YOU OR YOU CAN LET IT STRE

DO NOT GIVE UP, THE BEGINNING IS ALWAYS THE HARDEST.

It's not how many times you fall down. It's how many times you GET BACK UP.

I know I was BORN and I know that I'll DIE. The in-between is MINE.

IT'S HARD TO BEAT A PERSON THAT NEVER GIVES UP.

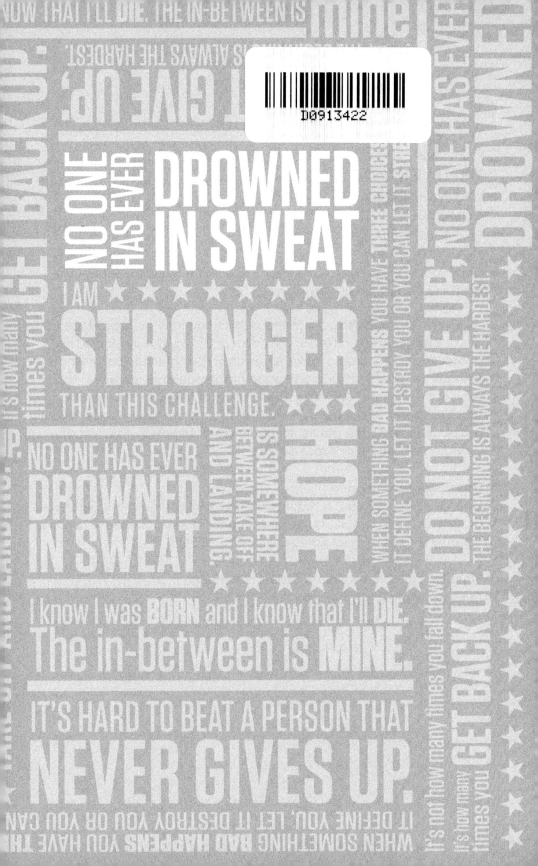

TIMOTHY & TITUS
226 Washington Ave N
Suite 300
Minneapolis, MN 55401

Copyright © 2016 by No One Ever Drowned in Sweat, G.R.I.T. – The Stuff of Leaders and Champions

All rights reserved. No part of this publication may be reproduced, distributed, or transmitted in any form or by any means, including photocopying, recording, or other electronic or mechanical methods, without the prior written permission of the publisher, except in the case of brief quotations embodied in critical reviews and certain other noncommercial uses permitted by copyright law. For permission requests, write to the publisher, addressed "Attention: Permissions Coordinator," at the address above.

Ordering Information:
Quantity sales. Special discounts are available on quantity purchases by corporations, associations, and others. For details, please contact Timothy & Titus Special Sales at 612-200-0888.

Manufactured in the United States of America
14 13 12 11 10 9 8 7 6 5 4 3 2 1

Dedication

Brooklyn, Bristol and Poppy,

Shun conventions,

Defy definitions,

Crush expectations,

Be hard to imitate,

Harder to impress,

And impossible to ignore.

Most importantly, don't be scared to live.

Acknowledgements

I would like to express my deepest appreciation to all those that have contributed to the book. Without you, the book would only be about a guy that no one really gives two shits about.

Table of Contents

Foreword

Bryan "Birdman aka Baby" Williams

Rapper, Record Producer, and
Co-Founder of Cash Money Records

G.R.I.T. Yeah, I know all about it. I am a successful performer and entrepreneur today, but my road to success has been a rough one and nothing was handed to me. My mom died when I was two years old and then my dad passed when I was five. I was in a boy's home, was homeless and grew up in the Magnolia Projects of New Orleans where I turned to selling drugs and robbery to make money to survive. I spent nearly two years in a correctional center for possession of marijuana and firearms before being acquitted.

Like Scott Petinga and others, I shouldn't have been a success – and I wouldn't have been if I had given up and conformed to the tragic life that dominated my formative years. But you see, I have the qualities Scott talks about in *No One Ever Drowned in Sweat: G.R.I.T. – The Stuff of Leaders and Champions.*

I have the *Guts* to take chances and move forward, whatever the cost, to make my dreams come true. I don't allow negative circumstances and people pull me down into complacency. I like the rewards of success and I've got the courage to chase it.

I have *Resilience* and don't take no for an answer. During the process of building my career and my business, Cash Money Records, I've been told "no" and "you can't" more times than you know, but I always find a way around NO, which is an unacceptable response if you believe in the person you represent.

I have *Initiative* and take the reins of my destiny in my own hands. I've never been the type to wait and see what somebody else has planned for me. I make my own way and, when success arrives, it is much sweeter.

I have *Tenacity* which has played a big role in my success as well as my survival. Coming from the south in the music business, I had to teach and educate myself. That resulted in pushing through a lot of mud while searching for the stars. In my business, many people see the lights, the microphone and the fame, but they don't see the label or really understand the struggle, so I've had to tenaciously educate executives and others along the way.

And the fight doesn't end when you become successful either. I understand Scott's struggle with cancer because my sister has it and I stand and fight with her every single day. Cancer is a bad scene and it takes G.R.I.T. to beat that monster back and overcome it.

When you have G.R.I.T., you weed out those that try to pull you down and you surround yourself with winners that have those same qualities. I have some great people in my life – Lil Wayne, Drake and Nicki Minaj – to name a few. And I greatly admire and respect others with G.R.I.T., like Scott Petinga, who aren't afraid to sweat and refuse to let the naysayers keep them from achieving their dreams.

May you have G.R.I.T. and the success it produces.

Bryan "Birdman aka Baby" Williams

Bonus

DISCOVERING YOUR ACTION MINDSET PROFILE

Scott Petinga, along with many other successful entrepreneurs, educators, sports heroes and experts, reveals in *No One Ever Drowned In Sweat* that it takes certain elements to effectively pursue and achieve goals, whether those targets are set for betterment in personal, business, or communal life arenas. He successfully shows that, in order to overcome life's hurdles and defeats, you must possess a certain type of mindset.

Scott isn't afraid to fail. As he admits, "I shouldn't be a success story. I've failed at almost everything I've ever tried; kicked out of the Marines, flunked out of school, fired from jobs, divorced... you name it, I've failed at it. But every success story starts from failure. Why? Because that's where all the learning happens."

Scott knows that individuals face variances in age, social and educational background, employment opportunity and other important factors that often make character development and achieving goals a widely different experience for each person. This understanding pressed him to create the **Action Mindset Profile** which is a valuable tool that you can use to gauge where you currently stand in accordance with the goals you desire to achieve. Scott often says, "To begin making real progress, you need to learn where you're most comfortable, most skilled and most proficient. Then move on and find a place where you feel the most uncomfortable, most uncertain and the most unsure of yourself. That's the first step."

MINDSET VS PERSONALITY

Let's explore these mindsets, but before we do, we need to first clarify the difference between a *Mindset* and a *Personality* trait.

Mindset: A preferred and adopted way of approaching life.

Personality: A wired way of acting and behaving based on genetics and environmental stimulation.

The difference: Mindset is a choice... Your CHOICE!

When you understand your preferences and defaults through your personal **Action Mindset Profile**, you begin to recognize the strengths and weaknesses associated with those preferences and you can make beneficial changes.

ACTION MINDSETS

There are four Action Mindsets that, when combined together, define the Action Mindset Profile. These are: Risk, Conflict, Decisiveness and Goal. Each of these mindsets is dichotomous, with two divergent preferences. Scott's profile consists of Guts, Resilience, Initiative, Tenacity (G.R.I.T.). What about yours?

Let's review these Action Mindsets:

Risk Mindset

This mindset highlights the boldness with which we pursue our passions versus a preference for what is known:

Guts: Being brave, courageous and willing to risk everything for a cause. People may bet against you, but you still pursue your goal and forge new paths along the way in order to achieve it.

Highlights: Boldness and Novelty

Versus...

Security: Preference for the road that will give you the best chance of achieving comfort and stability.

Highlights: Known and Proven Path

Conflict Mindset

The next mindset determines our willingness to welcome versus avoid failure:

Resilience: Knowing you may fail, but forge on. You see failure as a learning opportunity and embrace challenges rather than wallow in pity. You believe everything happens for a reason.

Highlights: Learning and Acceptance

Versus...

Assurance: If you know you are likely to fail at something, you will choose to avoid it. You opt for a route that is more likely to be successful and less likely to embrace conflict.

Highlights: Calculation and Avoidance

Decisiveness Mindset

The next mindset involves our desire for immediate action versus intense planning:

Initiative: Moving forward without hesitation. You see a goal and what needs to be done and you do it. You prefer action over waiting.

Highlights: Action and Movement

Versus...

Forecasting: Having a preference for planning and strategizing before action. You might weigh the pros and cons and develop a short, mid and long-term plan to guide your actions.

Highlights: Planning and Strategy

Goal Mindset

The final mindset focuses on the tendency to pursue identified goals passionately versus being diverted from goals for other purposes.

Tenacity: Even if your goal is in jeopardy, you are persistent and you keep pushing to see it through. You are determined and will not quit until your goal is reached.

Highlights: Perseverance and Passion

Versus...

Elasticity: Flexibility in the desire to achieve particular outcomes. You display a willingness to modify your goals, pursue the goals of others, or drop your goals altogether if too many obstacles are presented.

Highlights: Multi-tasking and Flexibility

Mindset Groups

Now that you understand the mindsets, you may also want to know how they interact. Action Mindset Profiles are grouped into four categories consisting of:

Guides: Those who show direction to others for achieving a vision.

Supporters: Those who work to ensure visions are achieved.

Capitalizers: Those who profit from a given vision.

Visionaries: Those who develop new visions to inspire others.

Mindset Group Table

The following table shows all possible Action Mindset Profiles with their associated Mindset group and a slogan for each type:

Mindset Group	**Action Mindset Profile**	**Slogan**
Guides	Ringmaster (SAIT)	The show must go on!
	Planner (SAFT)	Things must go according to plan!
	Head Coach (SRFT)	Practice makes perfect!
	Sherpa (SRIT)	I'll show you the way!
Supporters	Tinker (SAIE)	*I can help!*
	Citizen (SAFE)	Do what you should do!
	Advisor (SRFE)	I have an idea!
	Ninja (SRIE)	You're welcome!
Capitalizers	Day Trader (GAIE)	Play the odds! Sink or swim!
	Pundit (GAFE)	Let's talk about...
	Investor (GRFE)	Change when the situation changes!
	Streetfighter (GRIE)	Do whatever works!

Mindset Group	Action Mindset Profile	Slogan
Visionaries	Shark (GAIT)	I know what to do to succeed!
	Dreamer (GAFT)	Tomorrow will be better!
	Mastermind (GRFT)	Change the world!
	Trailblazer (GRIT)	Create your own path!

RESEARCH VS PRACTICE

Scott's initial identification of Action Mindsets was achieved through deep introspection about his own life experiences and what led him to be successful despite facing great odds. With this introspective foundation, he set out to confirm his hunches.

After testing different ways of assessing the Action Mindsets, he discovered that the insights he achieved from his personal experiences were shared and validated by hundreds of survey respondents whose mindset preferences accurately correlated with life outcomes. These included salary, recover from tragedy, level of education, entrepreneurial orientation, and likelihood of being an inventor.

You can also gain valuable insight into the elements of what makes you a success, or what blocks your path to becoming a success by taking the Action Mindset Profile.

You can discover more about your Action Mindset Profile, the outcomes of Scott's research and participate in shaping future research by becoming an Action Mindset member at www.knowyourmindset.com.

Introduction

BUT IT IS BROKE - LET'S FIX IT

We've all heard the adage, "if it ain't broke, don't fix it." But the mere suggestion that well enough is good enough is the reason Corporate America is itself broken.

I see ad campaigns that suck, salesman who can't sell shit, vendors focused on their own bottom-line, contractors that spend more time looking for work than actually working, managers who can't manage, leaders who won't lead—and that's just on my way into work!

I'm fucking amazed at the amount of incompetence, laziness, stupidity, backbiting and downright aggression I see in the marketplace every single day.

And it's not because I'm some fucking genius who's more perceptive than everybody else, far from it. I just tend to have a different paradigm because of who I am—and what I've been through.

I shouldn't be a success story. In the past, I've failed at everything I've ever tried. I graduated high school with under a 2.0 GPA, was prematurely discharged from the Marine Corps, was fired from or lost countless jobs, went through a divorce...

You name it and I've failed at it.

But every success story starts from failure.

Why? Because FAILURE is where the fucking learning happens!

I can't help it if Corporate America refuses to learn from its failures (and there are many), but you can learn from it, learn from mine and, more importantly, learn from your own.

Business as Unusual

Aside from all that failure—or maybe because of it—I still consider myself a pretty competent guy. The good news is that in a kingdom of incompetence, the competent guy is king!

Every day, I run into fucking assholes, clowns, dolts, wimps, losers and incompetents. Because of all that ineptness, I spend half my time educating people about how to ***run*** their own businesses, and that's before I can even begin to advise them on how to ***make*** things better.

Rules, politics, paradigm shifts, corporate culture, market sensitivity... it's all such bullshit! You know it, I know it, they know it, but most everybody's too afraid to admit it.

That's how companies work: the boss is never quite as smart as he thinks he is, managers get away with murder and we all just kind of "go along to get along", grabbing our paychecks until we move up the corporate ladder.

We put everything we've got into steadily climbing up that damned ladder, white-knuckling every rung, until we reach the pinnacle and we become the boss. And then, one day, we realize that we're stuck with the same fucking company we couldn't stand to work for on the way to the top.

However, by the time we have sufficient authority to change the situation, it's too late—everyone's too deep in the ruts of status quo. Good luck getting them the fuck out!

And to pull at one single thread in the fabric of most companies, or mess with the recipe, change the leadership, tweak the product, fine-tune the image, try something brave, fresh, or innovative, is liable to upset the apple cart, or at least a couple dozen investors.

So, it's business as usual, never business as *unusual*. Something that has real value—new and revolutionary—fraught with positive changes to embrace, is unheard of and to be avoided. Everyone is expected to adhere to the same cut and mold bullshit.

I say:

"Let me run my business my own fucking way!"

That's exactly what I did and continue to do.

My companies enjoy tremendous success, not because I micro-manage every minute of my employees' day, but because I mind my own fucking business and they mind theirs. Together, we use our skills and know-how to get the job done.

I am a "hands-free" boss at all my companies. I hire *brilliant* people to do *exceptional* work and then I do something really revolutionary. I let them alone to do it. It's just that simple, just that smart, just that revolutionary and just that effective.

The result? My first company, AQKURACY, was featured on Inc. magazine's 2012 list of the country's fastest-growing private companies.

But at the core, this book isn't about me, my companies, or even my competence. It's about you and what you can do to rise above creeping and soul-crushing mediocrity, ignore all the red flags and blaze your own fucking path to success.

Just Don't Let It Affect Your Work

So, okay, fine, Corporate America is broken. How the hell do you fix it?

Short answer: you can't, you never will, no one ever will on their own.

You have to start with the only person you can control and change: yourself.

Then make sure your world is the best it can be. Hopefully, your small change will inspire others to change and the spiral will become bigger until major change occurs throughout the business world.

That's how this works. That's how success works.

Individuals knowing their strengths, eliminating or honoring their weaknesses and using both to create their own unique success story in a world gone mad, sad and bland in its thinking about business and the road to success.

Life is fucking hard, change is hard, achieving success is hard, but it can be easier.

And that's what this book is about: making your success story easier.

Trust me. I hesitated a long time before writing a "self-help" book. *"They're all so worthless,"* I thought. All those authors spouting the same bullshit over and over, saying the same thing in different ways, coached by their media trainers, filtered down to sound just slightly different from the next guy, all the while telling you exactly the same thing: nothing.

At least nothing that is "earth-shattering", "life-changing", "brilliant", "illuminating", "overnight" or "instant", like the glowing endorsements on the book jacket promise to deliver.

Then, one day, I finally realized: the only one who *can* help me was looking back at me in the mirror every morning. The only one who has ever made a real difference in my life... was me.

Everybody will disappoint you and let you down at some point, sometimes unintentionally. Family members, lovers, spouses, friends, neighbors, celebrities, sports figures, politicians, employees, coworkers, supervisors and even those you consider mentors and leaders.

I'll never forget the day I first learned of my cancer diagnosis. I went into work numb from the news, sleepwalking into my boss's office to let him know what was going on in my life. And, okay, maybe to find a shoulder to cry on. I poured out my soul, voice shaky and fraught with emotion, hands trembling, expecting at least a *little* compassion.

Instead, he looked at me and said words I'll never forget:

"Just don't let it affect your work."

Walking out of his office that day I thought, *"Fuck you, I am my work!"* Why would anyone hire me otherwise? Everything I do makes up who I am. Everything that happens to me... where I go, what I go through and what it teaches me... it all contributes to who I am.

How could I not let something like cancer affect my work?

The strange thing is I didn't let it affect my work. My boss's cold and casual suggestion that day triggered something in me that allowed me to *be* even *more* me.

I realized that this boss, like nearly every other boss, teacher, professor, or senior military leader I'd ever encountered, didn't care anything about me... the special skills, qualities, or personality I brought to the job. They only cared about output, productivity and profit. They only cared about the bottom line.

I vowed that day to never be like that insensitive asshole and to move on to a better place.

It's Gonna Take G.R.I.T. to Succeed

It wasn't easy. All that self-help, mumbo-jumbo, feel-good crap only goes so far if you're not willing to "put boots on the ground", as they say in the Marines, and put it to good use.

It took a lot of head butting, cutting through red tape and simple self-sufficient maneuvering to start my own company three years later. And it seemed that the more I succeeded, the more challenges I faced.

The only difference now is that I've learned how to deal with them.

What I've learned is that it takes *G.R.I.T.* to succeed.

Not just the courageous, tough, decisive, never-say-die "grit" which defines our toughest, most successful, most badass men and women, but the acronym G.R.I.T. which describes what helped me succeed.

The G.R.I.T. I'm talking about consists of four important characteristics: Guts, Resilience, Initiative and Tenacity. It's going to be your secret ingredient for success as well.

Writing these words, I recall all the hard times, the down times, the tough times, the dark times and the lonely times that taught me this special skill set.

How I made it through them, I'm still not sure, but my goal is to make it so you learn G.R.I.T. before you go through such times yourself. You'll be better prepared than I was... and better prepared than the competition as well.

Don't just take it from me. I have the unique opportunity to network with some of the best thinkers, leaders, doers, movers, shakers and passionate people in the world today. They too fully realize that it was the elements of G.R.I.T. that got them to where they are. These success stories have learned to use and rely on Guts, Resilience, Initiative and Tenacity to overcome the doubts, fears, criticisms and other obstacles that stood in their way.

In this book, I will prominently feature thought-provoking insights from interviews that were conducted with notable CEOs, entrepreneurs, nonprofit heads, thought leaders, athletes, everyday heroes, academics and forward thinkers from all walks of life. Their words will be offered as quotes in the text as well as through nuggets of wisdom peppered throughout the book via sections entitled **TRUISM**, **TWO CENTS WORTH** and **NOTE**.

I'll share words of wisdom from bestselling authors like **Andy Paige**, author of *Style on a Shoestring*, **Chester Elton**, author of *The Carrot Principle*, and **Scot Anderson**, author of *Think Like a Billionaire*.

You will hear from athletes like soccer great Pelé and NBA standouts **Earl Monroe**, who played for the Baltimore Bullets and New York Knicks, and **Jonathan Bender**, who had an amazing comeback to professional basketball after developing a knee-strengthening brace that he designed to help his condition.

We'll gain insights from business leaders like **Scott Gerber**, Founder of Young Entrepreneur Council, **Randi Ilyse Roth,** a founding member of the Academy of Court-Appointed Masters (ACAM), and **Aaron Earls**, co-founder of Sports195.

Other highly successful people will add their words of wisdom like **John Katzman**, Founder of The Princeton Review and Founder & CEO of Noodle, **Billy Mann**, President of Global Artist Management for EMI, and **Zig Ziglar**, renowned author and motivational speaker.

You'll be inspired by people you may have never heard of before, who have not only succeeded in business, but in sharing their life lessons in building powerful organizations, charities and other nonprofits.

Folks like **Paul LeJoy**, a Cameroon immigrant who built a 75 million dollar business in seven years, will share how they think, live AND breathe success.

These and many other varied, but very influential, voices will all weigh in on the topic and components of G.R.I.T. and how it can help you succeed... in business and in life.

At the end of the book, I will feature an Adversity Scale which compares the attributes of G.R.I.T. we've learned from the interviews and see how you measure up.

Now sit down, grab a beverage and follow my mind-fucking journey on what makes successful people tick... what makes them succeed!

01

The G.R.I.T. Mindset

Chapter 1

TRUE G.R.I.T.

I like things that make you grit your teeth. I like tucking my chin in and sort of leading into the storm. I like that feeling. I like it a lot.

Daniel Day-Lewis – English actor

When you're a kid, life's all about the thrill. Climbing the tallest tree you can find, riding your bike as fast as you can, stomaching the tallest roller coaster, those are the things kids chase after. We were all fucking fearless!

Then when you grow up, it's about "playing it safe." So many times, we stop taking those exciting risks that come naturally as kids. That's why I love the "no fear" mentality of youth. My kids rip down the stairwell in a cardboard box with no forethought of the consequences. They make a decision and just go for it.

I think the problem with much of the leadership of many Fortune 1000 companies is that no one wants to make a decision. There is paralysis of indecision that grips the business world. Shit doesn't get done. No one is willing to put their ass on the line and take a risk. New ideas fail to emerge and complacency sets in which kills momentum.

When I was kid, I accidentally slit my wrist while playing near my house and almost bled to death. But did that stop me? Fuck no, that's what kids do! If they get hurt, they pick themselves up, dust themselves off, recover and continue to be daring.

I had "middle child syndrome" growing up, meaning I was motivated to do more to stand out. I had an inner drive that my older brother often lacked. Even though he was older and two grade levels ahead of me, we were often in the same classes. I had the G.R.I.T. to succeed and performed better than he did so I excelled faster and farther.

Be the First, Be the Best

My mother always had big plans for me. She wanted me to be the first in our family to go to college. The assumption was that you had to go to college to be successful.

I had other plans, however. I had met a Marine recruiter the summer prior to my senior year and, when the time to sign-up came, I needed my parent's permission to join being that I was only 17.

My dad had served in the Army and didn't hesitate to sign, but my mom was absolutely devastated that I was "throwing my life away" and she was reluctant to give her permission.

However, I'm persistent as a motherfucker and kept prodding her. She ultimately signed.

I guess that drive—the need to *prove myself*—is what led me to enlist in the Marine Corps in the first place. I picked the Marines because that branch of service was the most demanding–both mentally and physically.

Friends and family mocked me saying that I wasn't fit for the Marines. People like me, they said, joined the Air Force. Well, that just gave me another reason to prove the naysayers wrong.

From that point on, I got completely bored shitless with school. Even so, I didn't throw in the towel completely – I knew I needed to graduate, even if it was by the skin of my teeth, in order to ship off to boot camp come July. I hung in there and did what I needed to do in order to continue toward my goal.

Hell, the transition from high school to the Marines even proved to be a pain in the ass. A few weeks before shipping out, I was riding my bike into work and was hit by a drunk driver. It fucked me up pretty bad, but the Gulf War was in full swing and the Corps wanted me anyway.

So, off I went to boot camp freshly injured from a major accident. If you are even remotely familiar with the grueling schedule that they put recruits through then you know the pain I endured, especially through the first phase of the 13-week course which mostly consists of purposefully applied physical and mental suffering.

But you see, I've got G.R.I.T., so I kept going even though I had fractured bone fragments in my foot. It hurt like a son of a bitch and the doctors finally pulled me from training and put me into physical therapy. That really threatened to fuck up my plans.

You see, long-term plans are based on milestones and if you miss those milestones, your plans can go to shit quick.

In my case, I entered the Marines to pursue a career in military intelligence which would then lead to possibly getting accepted into the FBI or CIA.

I convinced my docs to let me take the upcoming physical fitness test even though I was hurt. I passed that bitch and was able to return to my original platoon.

Several months later, I thought I had fully recovered and could continue the pursuit of my goal as I entered Intel School. But fuck if I didn't get hurt again, which sent me back to physical therapy and caused me to miss the program. Bye, bye to that dream!

After that, I jumped through a host of frustrating hoops. The Corps wanted to send me to Japan to be a cook, but I ain't cook material so I refused.

Of course, Marine authorities aren't too fucking keen on you telling them "no" so they demoted me and shuffled me off to San Antonio to become a military policeman. I was okay with that, but I ended up flunking the physical exam due to having less than 20/20 eyesight.

So, what did those fuckers do? They demoted me again and tried to send me to Japan as a cook anyway. That whole dog-and-pony show was done on purpose to try and break my spirit so I would quit. I got demoted to the lowest rank possible and lost a lot of money, but I hung in there.

TRUISM

"Being successful", a phrase that has a different measure for every individual, is determined by each individual's goals or objectives in life. One of the many key ingredients to achieving one's success is based on DRIVE. It is my belief that there are three categories of drive that fit all people on this planet. They are: Natural Drive, Instilled Drive and No Drive.

Natural Drive is a category of drive that comes with birth. It is this type of drive that works similarly to a passion to compete. It keeps an individual going and motivates them to consistently seek the next level of achievement continuously. Some people are born with this type of drive, which makes them unique in their pursuit to success.

Instilled Drive is a category of drive that most people fall into. This type of drive is brought on when an individual is inspired by someone that is encouraging or pushing them to attempt to accomplish a certain or specific goal or objective. The overall goal may be reached by accomplishing several smaller goals towards the objective. The key factor in this type of drive is that it requires inspiration from another source or party. Unfortunately, once the goal has been achieved, a feeling of settling in can take over, unless new inspiration from someone steps in. Instilled drive can come and go in an individual's life without influences from others.

No Drive is a category of drive that seems to be increasing in America over recent years. This category of drive requires constant ways or methods to motivate and persuade individuals to seek some type of accomplishment, all with the intent to improve one's life or environment. Unfortunately, this type of drive may have a direct effect on many other people it may encounter. The effect can be positive in form of turning others to do just the opposite, causing them to fall into the instilled drive category. No drive can also effect people in the negative, meaning that it can lead individuals to thrive on not having any type of inspiration to improve themselves or their quality of life. Ultimately, this type of drive leads to a path of little to no success in life.

When thinking about the acronym G.R.I.T., both Natural and Instilled Drive work in support of its true meaning.

– Sergeant Major William H. Bly Jr.
United States Marine Corps Retired

What got me through all that shit was something I had seen as a kid. It was a picture of a big assed crane trying to swallow a frog that had a death grip on the crane's neck. The caption read: NEVER EVER GIVE UP! That image has been stuck in my head ever since.

I figured the Corps finally got what they wanted, though, when my grandfather passed away. They wouldn't grant me leave to attend the funeral so I went AWOL.

That and all the other seemingly trumped-up charges resulted in a court-martial where I was given an Other-Than-Honorable discharge which was neither dishonorable nor honorable, but it left me unable to draw any kind of military benefits. My time in service lasted a hard and frustrating 21 months and crushed my original dream.

I've got to say that in spite of all the bullshit, I loved the demanding environment of the Marine Corps. But through it all, I noticed that something was missing. In my opinion, the Corps lacked compassion and true sincerity, the same ingredients that I see missing in today's corporate world. The foundation used to be integrity, but it appears to have eroded significantly.

You can be a die-hard fanatic and still miss the mark in the sincerity arena. It was a suffocating routine, "purely by the numbers."

I Can Do That!

When I left the Marine Corps, I came home and got a city government job with the help of my dad who was 'connected.' Essentially, I was installing lights on police cars. I felt like I was wasting my talents and it wasn't exactly an exciting addition to my desired resume.

I found myself doodling and drawing illustrations in my free time to fight the boredom. I was supposed to be striking out into the unknown. You know, building a fucking adventurous career. Yet, here I was getting work that wasn't based upon what I was good at, but because I was my dad's son.

That was twenty plus years ago, when I was a young, starry-eyed kid who had recently returned from the Marine Corps. As fate would have it, I met William A. Cradle one summer day soon after and it truly was the impetus to who I am today. He took me in and got me started in the communication and graphic arts industry.

Bill saw me for what I was... a diamond in the rough. I was not educated or professionally trained, but I had the elements of G.R.I.T. I had guts, always found a way to be resilient, possessed a tremendous amount of initiative and oozed tenacity.

He mentored me, stoked my passion and allowed me to fail. He taught me that philanthropy is just as important (if not more so) as making money. And in the end when I wanted to explore other opportunities, he continued to remain a dedicated friend.

My G.R.I.T. was beginning to make a way for me.

> When I need to really pull through something and could use some powerful, yet simple, advice from someone who had unbelievable G.R.I.T., I look to those such as Gandhi who said, "Strength does not come from physical capacity. It comes from an indomitable will."
>
> ***– September Dohrmann – COO of CEO Space***

Moving On, Moving Up

The thing with me is I need to experience forward, upward movement in what I'm doing, both in my career and in my life. If things get boring and stagnant, I fucking move on to something else. I don't stop. I've never stopped.

Well, five years later, spanning several jobs and various geographies, I got an itch to further my skills and experience and wanted to move on. I accepted a position with a company in Charlotte, NC, but it didn't last long.

Prior to my arrival, my soon-to-be-boss was fired, the company was sold and the opportunity vanished. Poof!

I called up every single contact and followed through on every single lead I had in the metro. I didn't hear anything right away. Finally, after a couple of weeks, I got a call for a teaching position that was immediately available which helped to fill the void.

In the fall of 2000, I got my biggest break up to then via a call from J. Walter Thompson (JWT). The world's largest advertising agency was looking for someone to work for them for a 30-day period. It was a proposition that consisted of $10,000 in pay, free housing and all the food you can eat for a month's worth of work. I took the risk and I got the job-it lasted 21 months.

In the beginning, I was an interactive designer and eventually moved to account planning. In this position, I did a tremendous amount of work with Ford Motor Company. I helped develop ongoing dialogue that utilized multi-channel strategies illustrated Ford's commitment toward adding value to the ownership experience as well as to increase repeat and referral sales, and service retention.

Everything happens for a reason and this short time spent with that company was no different. I met phenomenal people and, even though we no longer work together, we are still in contact today.

Microsoft, Money and Mayhem

Shortly after leaving JWT, Microsoft wanted to hire me. They were one of the advertising clients I had previously worked with and they invited me to come on board with them in a full-time position.

However, during our discussion, they told me that over the next several years, I would be required to get an MBA degree "because everyone in the department had one." This rubbed me the wrong way. Why the fuck did I need an MBA? Considering I was already making a six-figure salary without one, doing the work and meeting the demands of the fast-paced, emerging technology industry, I was doing just fine. And so I turned their offer down.

TWO CENTS' WORTH

I didn't have that formal education. I didn't have that training. I didn't have a marketing background or experience. But the one thing I had going for me was a lot of perseverance and a strong work ethic. That can really take you far. And that, coupled with initiative and with courage and bravery... all those things together, it's amazing what can happen!

– Crystal Paine – founder of MoneySavingMom.com

So without hesitation I moved to Chicago and went to work for an agency that was the largest pre-print company in the U.S. That company produced most of the Sunday circulars across the country and my focus with them was on research and analytics.

During this period, I started courting my first wife. The agency had massive personnel turnover for months on end, all while I was getting involved in a serious relationship. I needed a position with more stability so I could take care of this woman with whom I wanted to marry.

So, I took a job with Santander Bank (formerly Sovereign Bank) in a small rural town 60 miles west of Philadelphia. What's more stable than the banking industry, right? Yeah, right. At least that's what I thought at the time.

While working at this fine establishment, I faced one of my biggest personal challenges—I was diagnosed with cancer. That news came one month after my wife and I were married. Life was trying once again to knock me on my ass.

During this time when I needed it the most, I discovered that my "phenomenal medical benefits" wasn't all that phenomenal. Like most health insurance that the majority of corporate 1000 companies provide, it consisted of high deductibles and bullshit coverage.

What I discovered during this period of personal turmoil was that a growing number of large companies have been turning to high deductible health plans (HDHPs) and "consumer-directed" health plans (CDHPs).

These types of insurance products are sold as reducing health care spending, yet they come with high deductibles which have been shown to only save plan owners in the very short-term[1]. Holders of such plans also tend to avoid the expense of preventative care and then discover, like I did, that chronic care coverage is both expensive and limited. The result is that early diagnosis of major health issues is thwarted and the cost is actually elevated[2].

As I reflected on my life, it didn't offer a very encouraging outlook. I was miserable at work, had a tremendous amount of debt and the corporate culture in which I was a mere cog was one of "decision-by-committee." I wanted to see true leadership or, at the very least, compassionate management. I saw neither.

I convinced my wife that if I got better after my treatment, I wanted to go back to the advertising world and see what could happen. I finally figured out that I wasn't cut out to spend my time in some boring "suit and tie" position. I just had too much creativity flowing around inside me to sit still for very long. It can be really easy to settle into a comfortable position in life, but G.R.I.T. allows you to break

(1) Haviland, Amelia M., et al (March 2015). *Do "Consumer-Directed" Health Plans Bend the Cost Curve Over Time?* Available from www.nber.org/papers/w21031

(2) Islam, Ifrad (October 2015), *Trouble Ahead for High Deductible Health.* Available from http://healthaffairs.org/blog/2015/10/07/trouble-ahead-for-high-deductible-health-plans/

free from those molds, leave your comfort zone and journey into the unknown in search of what you want to accomplish.

Eventually, I got better and called up my former employer, JWT, in Detroit and they told me they had openings in three cities: New York, Atlanta and Minneapolis. I took the position in Minnesota and we resettled in Minneapolis.

However, things didn't fucking work out for me there either. I was only at the organization for a few days before JWT decided to merge this office with a sister-agency and refocus its capabilities. It was basically the same thing that had happened in Charlotte, NC and, once again, what I thought was a positive opportunity vanished into thin air. It was time to move on to greener pastures.

When this occurred, my wife went to live with my parents for a brief time back on the east coast during the transition until I could figure things out. I went to work for a company as their Account Planning Manager. My duties with them consisted of analyzing a wide range of marketing data and performing qualitative research on consumer behavior.

During this period, I was introduced to a gentleman who was relocating from New York to the Twin Cities. He thought my background would be a good fit for his department, so he went on to introduce me to his boss at an award-winning agency. I was hired to be the company's Accountability Director and I flourished for one year with them, working for some of the world's most well-respected brands.

At first, I was extremely happy there because of my role, collaborating with talented colleagues and the thought of a $25,000 bonus if I could meet my key performance indicators. Fuck, I could so that. Besides, that amount was extremely important because my wife and I needed $25,000 for in vitro fertilization (IVF). You see, my cancer treatment also made me infertile and this was the only way possible that we could have our own biological children. The need was met... or so I fucking thought.

The problem was they refused to give it to me. Since the company I worked for was part of a global holding company, and some of the subsidiaries failed to hit their goals overall, the holding company instituted a freeze on hiring, salaries and bonuses.

Once again, the corporate world was throwing up hurdles to my success!

All In!

I was infuriated that somehow, somewhere, someone had made a decision based solely on fucked up economics. I generated almost five times my salary and compensation in that position and yet they couldn't afford to give me $25,000 to keep me happy, knowing damn well how important it was to us.

So I did what I do best, I quit. I didn't even have time to think about the consequences. I just fucking walked out the door.

My gut told me it was the right decision. It was like jumping out of an airplane and my first chute failed to open. I didn't panic, however.

I remained calm and called up my client at Harley-Davidson and negotiated a deal working directly for them.

The rest is history—the history of G.R.I.T. – forged in professional and personal adversity. That's why I talk about having **Guts**, being **Resilient**, applying **Initiative**, digging in with **Tenacity** and just going for it. I absolutely know it works because I have fucking done it myself!

Go after what you want and do what you believe in. But most importantly, believe in yourself.

Wayne Gretzky, the famous former Canadian NHL hockey player and head coach, said:

"You miss 100% of the shots you don't take."

If you don't take risks, you'll never know what the opportunities could have been. And I'm thinking that if you're reading this book then you don't want to live with the bumbling, stumbling triplets of "would've, could've, should've."

It is clear that nothing significant, nothing worthwhile, nothing innovative and nothing great ever comes without taking a risk.

The "NEXT BIG THING" never gets here without risk—a risk that maybe at first leads to failure—but at last, to success.

It will take G.R.I.T. to take those steps and see your way to the fucking end.

Chapter 2

A LITTLE ADVERSITY WON'T KILL YOU - DEVELOP SOME G.R.I.T.

All cultures through all time have constantly been engaged in a dance with new possibilities for life. Change is the one constant in human history.

Wade Davis – Canadian scientist, author, photographer

Okay, so I've been talking about having G.R.I.T., but what exactly is it? Merriam-Webster defines the word "grit" as a "firmness of mind or spirit: unyielding courage in the face of hardship or danger".

Now, that is definitely contained in what I am referring to, but my version of G.R.I.T. is an acronym that goes much deeper than that basic definition.

What I'm talking about is a set of characteristics that, when developed, will give you what it takes to overcome any obstacle that life can throw at you. It is a mindset for building the inner qualities needed to succeed... in business and in life.

G.R.I.T. is:

"G" – Guts – the internal super power which allows us to overcome adversity and steer a course over, under, around, or straight through life's many obstacles and challenges.

"R" – Resilience – the rebounding energy which allows us to bounce back from life's many defeats to enjoy the fruits of our labor and eventual success.

"I" – Initiative – the entrepreneurial spirit which inspires us to act on our biggest ideas and build a life—and career—for ourselves and by ourselves if need be.

"T" – Tenacity – the staying power which ultimately determines how hard we fight for our dreams.

G.R.I.T. – *Real simple to remember, real hard to live*

Developing G.R.I.T.

Life is fucking hard! I don't care who you are, where you live, or from what background you come. Even if you've grown up with a fucking silver spoon hanging out of your mouth, I guarantee that you have gone through, are going through, or will go through some tough times that will damn near make you throw your hands up in surrender.

But surrendering doesn't win battles, much less the war. If you're going to outlast that son of a bitch, whether it's one person, a group of people, or a situation, you've got to have more G.R.I.T. than they do.

Champions are made from a consistent stream of learning, preparing, getting out there where the fight is and, if knocked down, getting back up and going again. Sure, you may lose a battle and get your ass whipped, but that doesn't mean you're defeated. You learn from the experience, get up and dust yourself off, and strike out again.

If you quit, however, you neither win nor truly live.

NOTE

> Life is all about risk. Risk is inherent in every step along the way, in every decision, in every choice to move forward, whether it's to overcome an obstacle or to achieve a dream.
>
> True grit is not for the faint of heart. It takes trust and guts to push through the fear and to jump over that gap to success. Without it – it being that "oomph"... the

> guts it takes to push through the unknown – success will always remain beyond our reach.
>
> *– Linda Losey – Entrepreneur, Owner of Bloomery Plantation Distillery, Best-selling Author & Award-winning Artist*

What you need to do to become as successful as you possibly can is to develop G.R.I.T. and I'm going to help you do that through this book. Contained within each one of the four components of my system are four characteristics, or traits, that I will point out along the way.

These traits are the essence of each aspect of G.R.I.T. and, when focused upon and developed, become the rock solid foundation you need to succeed... in every arena of life.

The First Step

Before you strike out to slay giants, you have to do something.

The first step in obtaining G.R.I.T. is to honestly assess yourself and discover where you're the most comfortable, most skilled and most proficient. Then step right past that to a place where you feel the most uncomfortable, the most ill at ease and the most unsure of yourself.

Why? Because you might fucking fail and that's exactly where the learning and growth happens.

The majority of people are defeated before they even get out there to face the fight. In their minds, they make mountains out of mole hills and giants out of shadows. They refuse to leave the security of their comfort zones and take the risk of failing that comes with doing so.

Hell, even if your situation really is a nasty giant, there are multiple stories throughout history of people overcoming seemingly insurmountable odds just because they got out there, kept pressing forward and eventually won the day... they had G.R.I.T.!

So, you have to be willing to get your ass up and step into the unknown towards your dreams and goals. That is the ONLY way to obtain what you want for your life.

TWO CENTS' WORTH

> Failure is not the end of everything, but the beginning of something greater!
>
> ***– Brenda Coffman – founder and CEO of Blondie's Cookies Inc.***

I guarantee that if you choose to stay in your comfortable, little "happy place" then you will not reach your goals or realize your dream.

However, I believe that you at least have a desire to achieve success, if not a burning bosom of fire just itching to find some direction and get the ball rolling. My G.R.I.T. mindset is the answer to fulfilling both.

The Takeaway

The hallways in my home and office are lined with quotes, sayings, musings, proverbs and adages. Some are fancy and framed, like artwork. Some are tiles, mortarboards, printouts, or posters. Some are merely scraps of paper, sticky notes, or cutouts from magazines.

I absolutely fucking love word porn. The wisdom of others—writers, thinkers, doers, inventors, CEOs, priests, rabbis, missionaries, coaches, actors, directors and just generally smart, wise and funny people—is what inspires me to try new things, take new risks, follow new directions, or simply get off my ass and get going.

The quote I'd like to share that covers the theme of this section is a simple one by Neale Donald Walsch:

"Life begins at the end of your comfort zone."

I live by that quote. Not because I don't enjoy comfort, but because I know complacency kills.

I get tired like everybody else. I work long hours and often, at the end of what feels like a never-ending day battling inadequacy in the corporate world, I think, "Why the fuck am I doing this? Why don't I just cash in all my chips, retire early and go sit on a beach somewhere... no worries in the world."

Beyond the obvious, where's the fun in that? I don't do this for the money. Success is a challenge and challenge always requires change. And change is the single most uncomfortable thing in the human condition.

Change is also the fire that forges greatness. Without change, I'd still be the broken down, in both body and spirit, and flat-broke failure I was years ago. Without change, I never would have met my first wife, started a company, attained success, had three beautiful daughters or met wonderful, vibrant, confident colleagues and coworkers. I never would have started a handful of foundations raising millions of dollars for a variety of worthy causes, or written a single word of this book.

My challenging, frustrating, wonderful, unique, confusing and complicated life is beautiful because of change and yours can be too. You just have to find *comfort* in the *uncomfortable*.

Sounds easy, right? Well, it fucking isn't, not at first anyway, but it gets easier. In fact, it's quite addictive. Once you discover the joys of discomfort and the ROI of risk taking, you will become as addicted to change as you once were to conformity, simplicity, boredom and the status quo.

And your first step toward change is turning the page, because that is where your journey to greatness begins.

Chapter 3

THERE'S NO DEGREE FOR G.R.I.T.

Formal education will make you a living;
self-education will make you a fortune.

Jim Rohn – American entrepreneur, author, motivational speaker

Jim Rohn was a self-made millionaire who rose through the ranks to realize his dreams. He started his life journey working for Sears as a stock clerk. He then had several mentors that took him under their wings and taught him valuable lessons of life.

Rohn's G.R.I.T. and those lessons led Rohn to become a success of his own as well as go on to mentor such successes as Herbalife founder Mark Hughes and famous motivational speaker Tony Robbins.
Rohn himself received the CPAE Award from the National Speakers Association in 1985.

Today's corporate world is floundering and failing in areas across the board and, in my opinion, it is because they have left the sweet waters that bubble forth from people with natural G.R.I.T. and have herded around themselves those that have obtained a stamped degree from some robotic university.

> Formal education isn't real world and never will be. It has merit, but without initiative all the formal education in the world means nothing. The real education starts AFTER the initiative kicks in to get out there and actually take action.
>
> ***– Rick Hinnant – Entrepreneur & Co-Founder (with wife Melissa) of Grace & Lace***

Formal education is all well and good, but it plays an extremely small role, if any, when it comes to meeting goals and fulfilling dreams. Furthermore, it has left millions of Americans bogged down in debt which can be a dream-killer!

Andy Paige is a beauty and style expert, TV personality, entrepreneur and author of the bestseller *Style on a Shoestring*. During our interview, Andy provided a glimpse of her formal education experience that is all too common in mainstream America. She said:

I come from a dirt road in Alabama and I was a high school dropout. I dropped out of high school and moved to New York at 17 with $300. I was so afraid of being that idiot high school dropout from Alabama that I over-educated myself to compensate for my fear of being considered an idiot, my fear of not being good enough and my fear of not being able to walk into a room and being taken seriously.

I thought that if I had a really, really stellar education that somehow it would make up for all of these shortcomings. And

I put myself in great financial peril. And it was a big mistake.

Reading the right books, networking, being curious and being a constant human student are far more important than putting yourself in debt with a formal education. Let me tell you that right now.

When it comes down to it and the day is done, it is the inner workings of G.R.I.T. that wins the day... not a head full of babblings, a piece of fancy parchment and a mountain of debt.

Education – Not a Requirement

A whole lot of people have little to no idea what I'm talking about when I say being successful doesn't require a formal education. Unless folks have come to a certain place of maturity in their lives to see the value of what I'm talking about then they tend to look at me like a deer caught in the headlights.

Formal training most definitely has its place, especially in vocational fields, that is essential to becoming an effective electrician, mechanic, carpenter, etc., or in highly sophisticated careers such as a physician, psychologist and other professions requiring detailed learning.

TWO CENTS' WORTH

You can educate yourself along the way, but without initiative you will never get started.

> There is something to learn from nearly everyone you come in contact with. I have learned from my parents, my peers, my customers. Every day brings opportunity to learn from someone.
>
> ***– Rebecca Rescate – Founder of CitiKitty & Rebecca Rescate Inc. & Co-Founder of HoodiePillow***

What I am saying is that a large portion of formal education is a vast waste of both time and money. Before our society began emphasizing formal education, most of the movers and shakers were self-made. Even in recent times, a large portion of major accomplishments have been made by self-made men and women.

The list of self-made success stories that did not pursue, did not have the means for, or were denied a formal education is a long one. Here are just a few examples:

- Alfred Nobel – Chemist, engineer, inventor, scientist, business leader. Used his fortune to establish the Nobel Prizes. Only attended an organized school as a child for 18 months. Mostly private tutors. Did not attend college.
- John D. Rockefeller, Sr. – Entrepreneur, CEO, business leader. Became one of the world's richest men. High school dropout.
- Coco Chanel – Fashion designer. Taught to sew by nuns after her father placed her in an orphanage as a child. No formal training.

- Thomas Edison – Inventor. Held over 1,000 patents. Completed 3 months of high school. Mainly home-schooled.
- Wright Brothers – Inventors. Credited with inventing the first successful airplane. Never graduated high school.
- Albert Einstein – Theoretical physicist. High school dropout. He tried to enter the Swiss Federal Polytechnic College in Zurich, but failed the entrance exams.
- Bill Gates – Computer programmer, entrepreneur, author. Creator of Microsoft. Dropped out after two years at Harvard.
- Steve Jobs – Technology inventor, entrepreneur. Creator of Apple. Dropped out after one year at Reed College.
- Mark Zuckerberg – Computer programmer, entrepreneur, philanthropist. Creator of Facebook. Dropped out after two years at Harvard.
- Jennifer Lopez – Dancer, singer, actress. Did not attend college.
- Walt Disney – Founder of Walt Disney Company. High school dropout.

- Rachael Ray – Author, businesswoman, cooking TV show star. Never attended college. No formal culinary training.

Again, this is just a partial list of ultra-successful people that relied on their G.R.I.T. instead of education to meet their goals, fulfill their dreams and change the world.

G.R.I.T. vs. Formal Education

Perhaps you need more convincing that you already have the raw materials to do whatever you want in your life without spending the time and money to earn a degree that more than likely will have nothing to do with meeting your goals.

I am a stickler for this subject because I lack formal education and the degree it eventually produces which is fucking thrown in my face time and time again by corporate dicks. I've been denied positions and told I'd never amount to anything without it.

TRUISM

I've known people who have great education, but they lack the willpower or the spirit to reach for their goals. They don't push, they don't ask more of life, or they don't push themselves more.

I think it's that initiative, that drive, that willingness to succeed – I describe it as an internal fire or internal hunger – however you define it, that is what makes

> all the difference. I mean, it's there or it's not. Education doesn't buy that for you.
>
> ***– Ines Temple – President of LHH – DBM Peru & LHH Chile, President of CARE Peru and author of Usted S.A. Empleabilidad y Marketing Personal***

Was I the only one who became a big success without a formal education? I was curious, so this question was presented during the interviews of highly successful people that were conducted for this book.

Would you choose (an element of G.R.I.T.) over a formal education? If so, why?

Here are some of the responses:

Randi Ilyse Roth is a founding member of the Academy of Court-Appointed Masters (ACAM). As a lawyer, she was a primary author of the original 2006 version of the ACAM bench book, *Appointing Special Masters and Other Judicial Adjuncts: A Handbook for Judges.*

When asked which she would choose, Randi responded:

> If I had to pick, I'd pick guts. The reason I'd pick guts is that with guts and no formal education, you can still make a huge impact in this world. With formal education and no guts, you may be okay, but you are less likely to strive for and achieve impact. By impact, I mean impact in the world of work and/or

> service and also impact in the realm of foregoing authentic, loving, life-giving relationships.

Randi clearly associates **Guts** with not only impacting the business world, but also for creating strong relationships in other arenas of life.

When it comes to **Resilience**, Pastor Andy Thompson made his choice clear when he answered:

> Formal education is something that can be attained by almost anyone and achieved with varying amounts of effort. Resilience, on the other hand, seems to be an innate trait that some people show that requires a substantial amount of effort. For those reasons, I would choose resilience.

Fleetwood Hicks is the President and Founder of Villy Custom, a company that produces luxury custom cruising bicycles, fashion wear and accessories. Fleetwood said:

> Personally, I feel that education is extremely overrated when it comes to really going out and getting the work done. I look for people that have initiative, the attitude. I think you can always train anybody with a good attitude and initiative. You can train them, teach them and they can learn by being around you or whatever, but they've got to have the initiative to do a good job.

Michelle Patterson, President of Global Women Foundation and Founder, President and CEO of Women Network LLC, responded by saying:

> There's nothing more valuable than going through the experiences... and sometimes really tough experiences... where you get out the other side and you appreciate going through that experience because it shaped you, it made you stronger. Then you're able to go ahead and share that experience and you went through to help other people.
>
> We all have our stories. We all have those experiences and I think that's the journey through life which is to be able to go ahead and have those experiences. Just falling down, getting back up, falling down again, getting back up, not giving up, but having the perseverance to keep pushing through when you are having those experiences.
>
> You can't get that from a formalized education, school training.

Scot Anderson, motivational speaker, executive coach and Christian comedian, chose tenacity over formal education. He had this to say about it:

> I would choose tenacity all day long. Now, I mean, I have a college degree. I have a mathematics degree. The only thing that I learned in college, I believe, would be dedication... tenacity. That's what I believe

> I learned in college through all the classes and everything. Most of them were just a waste of my time. But what college taught me was to stick through it, keep working hard and give your best. You don't do well on a test? You've got to come back and do better on the next test.

> I would definitely choose initiative over formal education and training because I can train you to do what I need you to do here. And it would be the way I want it done, which is the right way!
>
> ***– Kim Nelson – Founder of Daisy Cakes***

Model, actress and producer Halle Berry seemed to have a similar take on her stint in college. Halle is quoted as saying:

"By the time I left school, I had a lot of tenacity."

By the way, Halle dropped out of school where she was pursuing a degree for news reporting and applied her G.R.I.T. to her dream of entertaining. That seems to have worked out quite well for her!

In my opinion, acquiring a degree involves a shitload of wasted time and money on something that can be obtained without it. In a lot of cases, those years spent pursuing a degree actually produces the wrong fucking career. A lot of people come to this conclusion and change horses in mid stream AFTER they've wasted all that time and money.

The Takeaway

In some respects, formal education is fine and dandy. Certain careers benefit from or require gaining accumulated knowledge, both from a legal and performance view. As mentioned before, there are some things that can be learned and learned more proficiently and rapidly than if you try going it on your own.

However, when it comes to the qualities that it takes to actually fulfill dreams and achieve goals... when it comes to having G.R.I.T.... it can be a waste of time, energy and money seeking a degree.

This is especially true today. Society is flooded with people that have sacrificed a great deal to get that Almighty Degree who are flipping hamburgers, driving taxis, or working at some other menial bullshit job because their field of training has been saturated, or someone else has a few more fucking alphabets to impress the corporate assholes, or that other person simply has more G.R.I.T.

On top of that, universities are steeply raising their financial fees, increasing the levels of both student and facility debt and producing a lower quality of graduate[(3)].

(3) The Economist (December 1, 2012). Not What It Used to Be: American Universities Represent Declining Value for Money to Their Students. Available from http://www.economist.com/news/united-states/21567373-american-universities-represent-declining-value-money-their-students-not-what-it

Award winning novelist Omar Tyree sums it up pretty well by saying:

> Education is all around you. I can't even name all of the people that I have learned from. You simply have to keep your eyes open and your mind focused to catch good tactics, strategies and executions that are all around you.
>
> As a writer, I learn something new to write about every day. So my trade keeps me curious and inspired. Curious and inspired people are always learning. Everyone should want to know more and want to do more until they are no longer on this earth. Otherwise, you're wasting away your life.
>
> Do you want to realize your dreams, make a difference in the world and live a fulfilled life? I am happy to tell you that you that G.R.I.T. is what it takes to achieve your goals, regardless if you choose to get a formal education or not.

Read on to find out how you can develop the foundational essences of G.R.I.T.

02

G is for GUTS

Chapter 4

THE FOUR TRAITS OF GUTS

Who am I not to be a mover and shaker? Who am I not to shake my own little world?

Paul LeJoy - author, entrepreneur

Guts. We are accustomed to hearing how someone has the "guts" to do this or that, but we tend to accept such a term and move right along without really questioning the meaning.

So, what exactly is **Guts** anyway? Is it an inherent ability to persevere and overcome life's adversities? Or do you develop guts over time as difficulties press in on you?

Is sheer endurance forged just by flat outlasting all the crap that life throws at you? Is that **Guts**?

That is definitely a part of it. Paul LeJoy, quoted above, is a fine example. Although he is a successful entrepreneur and author today, Paul grew up in Cameroon, Africa, where he was often beaten for being late to school after having walked nearly five miles to get there... by his teacher! To keep returning under such threats and conditions in hope of escaping poverty will press some fucking **Guts** into you.

If **Guts** are forged through such difficulties then why do so many people who talk about persistence crumble at the slightest sign of trouble, challenge, conflict, confrontation, or adversity that have lives much easier than LeJoy's?

The answer is a fairly simple one. Most of us need to see proof that we will succeed before we take the risk. We want solid, hard evidence that we can hold in our hands, or view as a progress chart showing growth stats.

We need to see how something can help us before we'll fully invest in it. Then, before we invest, even in an emotion, we want to know that there will be a return on that investment.

I'm presenting to you in this chapter my own burden of proof that having **Guts** produces fucking results. But how, exactly, will you benefit from having **Guts**? What's in it for you? We're all busy, right? Why go out of your way to develop a skill, habit, or trait if there's no fucking significant ROI?

In this chapter, I'm going to identify four major attributes of Guts and, with the help of a few friends, colleagues, business superstars and entrepreneurial leaders, I'm going to show you just how valuable these traits are.

Put 'em together and you've got **Guts**.

TWO CENTS' WORTH

> Guts is HUGE! Business is the great unknown with so many different pieces and facets. No one ever knows what the next day may bring, so you have to have tremendous guts to face and conquer the challenges ahead.
>
> *– Rick Hinnant – Entrepreneur & Co-Founder (with wife Melissa) of Grace & Lace*

Trait One: *Decisiveness*

One thing that **Guts** helps you to do is break free from fear and to make decisions with more confidence.

Basketball legend, entrepreneur and inventor Jonathan Bender understands this from experience. Upon entering the NBA in 1999 as the number five overall draft pick, Jonathan soon realized that a painful growth spurt he suffered during childhood was haunting him at the onset of fulfilling his dream. He was plagued by cartilage damage and other knee problems shortly after his entrance in the NBA.

Desperate to take pressure off his knees, he engineered his own apparatus using a few supplies he picked up at a drugstore. Through trial and error, he successfully created a series of bands running from his waist down to his Achilles tendon, all attached by a harness and stirrup.

The prototype proved to relieve Jonathan's pain which prompted him to put the product in motion for mass distribution.

His design tested remarkably well in a biomechanical analysis performed at Purdue University. His product is now available on the market as the JBIT MedPro.

Although Jonathan's problems brought an early end to his aspiring NBA career, he refused to be defeated, mustered up some fucking **Guts** and took another route to become a success.

Bender describes **Guts** as being *all in*. He says:

> It's that moment or feeling where you know nothing can make you think, say, or do otherwise. It is almost a form of having tunnel vision in the sense that there is no amount of reason or logic that could surpass your decisiveness.

Imagine being so decisive that fear is an afterthought, not your default, "go to" emotion. Too often, we let fear rule our lives rather than taking control of situations and commanding the outcomes we desire, even if we have to take an alternative route to get there. This is known as the amygdala hijack, a phrase coined by Daniel Goleman in his book *Emotional Intelligence: Why It Can Matter More Than IQ* published in 1996. The amygdala is emotional center of the brain from where stems the trigger point of the human fight, flight, or freeze response[4]. G.R.I.T. can help prevent you from being hijacked by your natural emotional responses.

The first trait of **Guts**, therefore, is being able to banish the fear and embrace decisiveness.

Trait Two: *Clarity*

Having **Guts** gives you clarity which, in turn, allows you to make decisions more quickly and decisively. It's easy to make rapid decisions, but much harder to make good decisions quickly.

Clarity does that for you. It gives you the vision to see not only how a certain decision might affect you right now, but also how it might play out in the future.

From my experience, this is a HUGE differentiator... both in business and in life. You don't always have to see the outcomes and, sometimes when you step out boldly, you DON'T see the outcomes, at least those that are long-term.

However, having **Guts** doesn't mean you launch out without a plan. No. You fucking need a plan to follow towards your

(4) McKeever, Monty (May 18, 2011). *Tricycle. The Brain and Emotional Intelligence: An Interview with Daniel Goleman.* Available from http://tricycle.org/trikedaily/brain-and-emotional-intelligence-interview-daniel-goleman/

goals. Having **Guts** means you create a vision and then you take the steps to bring that bastard to fruition!

Making a decision that is good for today doesn't always bode well for tomorrow, the next day, the next year, or the next decade. There are multiple variables that can pop up along the way that will force you to change your plans, or impact your desired outcome.

You have to be able to make decisions "mid-stream" if you want to control damage and keep momentum flowing toward your goal.

True clarity offers you a 360-degree view of a decision, from top to bottom, side-to-side, backward and forward, and over again. But it takes **Guts** to commit to such a 3-D rendering of the future and admit that what looks good today might not be in your best interest tomorrow.

Trait Three: *Boldness*

That brings us to the third trait of **Guts**... boldness.

Folks tend to settle into places where they feel comfortable, not only in careers, but in personal and professional alliances as well.

If you're unsure, anxious, or fearful, you will tend to hang out with others that are also unsure, anxious and fearful. It's the old "birds of a feather" thing. You strive for less, because that feels better. Less effort means a fucking lot less stress and less accountability and surrounding yourself with like-minded people eases the pain of the process.

However, once you have settled into your comfy spot, the act of striving beyond it can place you outside the zone of mediocrity which grows increasingly frightening the longer you remain there. Furthermore, you aren't motivated to press forward because you've got a bunch of the same types of mediocre people around you that don't want to rock the boat and leave their comfort zones.

However, when you are bold – in essence, when you have **Guts** – you tend to cluster around other confident and brave people. You feed off their energy as well as bring reciprocal energy to those relationships, all of which creates a natural springboard of action.

When you take a bold step onto the path of fulfilling your goals and surround yourself with gutsy people, you operate at another level, one that is high above that of your former mediocrity. Bold, gutsy people challenge you to be even bolder and gutsier, causing you to challenge yourself, avoid mediocrity altogether and blast off towards levels of success you never dreamed possible.

Boldness breeds boldness and this quality comes from the recesses of **Guts**!

> To have major breakthroughs, guts is everything. If you don't push that next boundary, if you don't push through your comfort zone, you're stuck where are.
>
> So, if you can't get comfortable then do it!
>
> You have to have the guts to push the boundary of your own comfort zone and, when you do that, the doors open. You have to have the guts to challenge yourself to that next level.
>
> ***– Dan Rothwell – Entrepreneur & Electrical Engineer***

Trait Four: *The Power to Invent*

When you have **Guts**, you not only possess the ability to make decisions clearly and the boldness to step out and fulfill them, you also possess an incredible power... the power to invent (or reinvent) your life.

Randi Ilyse Roth shared a personal story with us about **Guts**. It goes like this:

> I have a story about my daughter, Annie. She was a very shy child. When she was in about 3rd grade, she invented a holiday for her school: Lime Green Day. On May 27 of each year, she tried to get each person in her school to wear lime green. Oddly, it largely worked.

> At the school assembly on the afternoon of Lime Green Day, in front of about 200 parents and students, one mother asked my painfully shy daughter, "Annie, did you make this up or is it real?" Annie, who I thought would be terrified to speak, thought about it for a moment, and then stood up in front of the entire assembly and said, "I made it up and it's real."

Annie's story is a great example of this fourth trait of **Guts**. Quite often, as entrepreneurs, we are in a mad rush to succeed rather than taking the fucking time to create something new and original. We simply reinvent what has already succeeded beforehand.

While there's nothing wrong with tweaking an existing idea and making it your own, especially if it's already highly successful, it takes fucking **Guts**, and lots of 'em, to create something entirely new.

The question now becomes; do you have enough **Guts** to read on? If you do, you'll discover how true G.R.I.T. can change your life.

Chapter 5

COURAGE COMES FROM WITHIN

Courage is rightly considered the foremost of virtues, for upon it all others depend.

Winston Churchill – British Prime Minister, statesman, writer

These opening words by former U.K. Prime Minister Winston Churchill reveal how courage, or **Guts**, is the foundational essence of all other success qualities.

If you don't have a solid stream of courage bubbling forth from your internal well then all the other attributes of G.R.I.T. won't withstand the test of time or hold up against life's fiery trials.

The greatest enemy of success is fear. The diabolical devil of fear is what rises up before us, issues screams of defeat in our faces and causes us to back down, give up, or never fucking try at all.

Franklin D. Roosevelt understood fear. He was elected president of the United States during the Great Depression and led the nation out of a black hole of despair and back to a state of booming prosperity. FDR famously said:

"The only thing we have to fear is fear itself."

That statement is truer than most realize. FDR didn't allow fear to stop him from helping the country overcome the worst financial disaster in its history.

On the other side of the coin, cowardice is the lack of courage to face fear and the danger it brings, whether real or imagined. If you don't face those dark battles in life, then you are already defeated before you ever begin.

Even if you muster up the **Guts** to get your journey started, if you allow upcoming fears to stop you along the way then you are still just as defeated as if you hadn't set out in the first place.

The battles of life come one after another and if you quit fighting, if you quit forging ahead and return to your comfy place, you will never realize your dreams. On top of it all, you will feel like shit when all those victory stories are being told by those who have braved the battles.

When things get dark and dreary, and it looks like there is nothing but defeat ahead, it takes **Guts** to stand upright, charge into the abyss and fucking walk away victorious.

Could you be defeated? Of course you could! But you are most certainly defeated if you don't try. If you don't have **Guts**, you will never know the sweet taste of victory that comes when you slay the dragon.

Personal Goals

I've been painting a picture of courage needed to win big battles, but it takes just as much courage to achieve personal goals, regardless of their size.

There are lots of self-help books out there that give all kinds of magic formulas and offer supposedly secret tips to meeting personal goals, but I'm here to tell you in this book that it takes nothing more than G.R.I.T. And the foundational part of my mindset is simply having **Guts**!

All of my life, I have listened to people bitch, moan and complain about things in their lives. But what actions do these people take to contribute to those things they want to see changed? Zip! Zilch! Absolutely fucking NADA!

If all you are going to do is sit around and complain about things without making plans, setting goals and taking action to do something about them then get your ass out of the way and let us movers, shakers and doers pass on by and get the fucking job done!

Successful people don't cower in the corner because they know that the only way to see their dreams come true is to get out there and make them happen.

Just ask John Frederick (Jay) Jones. He's a successful attorney, entrepreneur and owner of Jones Scones. He told me:

> Fear is the number one killer of dreams. As soon as you learn that, you're going to have to face your fears in order to move forward in any endeavor.
>
> How do you move forward with this? Well, your limits are all self-made. Your limits are purely self-defined. So, if you're able to push through the fear and have the discipline to keep working intelligently and hopefully efficiently, you're going to be able to get anything done.
>
> Guts is facing fear. You have to accept that. I know you're scared. Do it anyway.

Fulfilled dreams are born out of vision and the only way to achieve what you see in your mind... to bring that vision into reality... is to take the steps necessary to get it done.

The "Magic" Is Action

If you're looking for a magic formula to success, then you need a fucking fairy or a lousy leprechaun... and good luck finding one of those!

But if you want to experience the real deal of fulfilling your dreams and desires, you have to put your hand to the plow and start digging up the dirt. You're going get dirty, you're going to sweat, you're going to cuss and you're probably going to cry and bleed some along the way.

However, if you don't muster up some courage and take the steps necessary to reach your goals then you're still going to be sitting on your ass watching life and others pass you by.

If you've got the courage to create a vision of success, then you best have the courage to see it through. It may not happen just the way you have pictured in your mind, but if you keep plugging away then you will eventually reach your destination... one way or another. That's what G.R.I.T. does. It gets you to your goals come hell or high water.

What you have to do is to get it in your head that there is no fucking magical formula. Success comes from having G.R.I.T. and that starts with having the **Guts** to step out and get the ball rolling... despite any fears or doubts from your own mind or from the naysayers.

TRUISM

> I think you have to, first of all, not only be courageous, but a bit crazy also to just leave behind a paying job and start your own business not knowing when in the world you'll ever get paid again. You've got to pay the bills and you've got to pay the employees and the taxes and the insurance and everything that goes along with owning your own business.

> Sometimes, you have to bluff a little, even to yourself. You just have to put on blinders and go with your gut and go with your wherewithal and make something happen and make the business successful.
>
> *– Kim Nelson – Founder of Daisy Cakes*

Slay Negativity

Most people don't ever take that initial step of fulfilling their goals because they are defeated internally by their own damned feelings. Emotions can be some of the biggest, nastiest barriers we have to confront on our way to achieving our goals.

What the majority of people don't realize is that emotions are a direct result of thoughts. The reason folks don't recognize this is that they treat feelings as fact. "I feel like a loser, therefore I am!" or "I can't do it, therefore I won't even try!"

People tend to dwell on these types of feelings and are convinced that they are true without ever raising the courage to prove them wrong. Those folks are called average and mediocre and they are defeated by their own thoughts without hardly any outside resistance.

In keeping with the discussion of this book, let's look at an example of this. While reading about courage to realize your dream and reach your goal, you think to yourself "I want to be a millionaire."

What is the next thought that pops into your head? In most cases, it is probably "I can't do that!" That thought is then immediately followed by a feeling of overwhelming fear, doubt and other nasty negative emotions that convinces you not to even try.

Now, that's an extreme example, but it works the same on every level of human existence. You could just as easily entertain the thought of "I want to start my own business", but then a series of negative thoughts pummel you with things like "Think of all that paperwork! I don't know where to begin!", "Nobody is going to back my idea!", or "I don't have the time to invest!"

Following right on the heels of these kinds of negative thoughts are those nasty fucking feelings of fear and doubt which can make you give up before any actions have been taken.

Nick and Elyse Oleksak took an idea Nick had of selling cream cheese stuffed bagel balls, added a food mixer and a pastry gun, and created the highly successful business of Bantam Bagels. During our interview, they told me:

> Elyse: We talk about how we don't know how this happened, or where it even came from, but we drive our business with this absolute blind belief in ourselves and in our product.
>
> You have to believe in your product. You can't be half-hearted about what you're trying to build,

> literally. We've always had this entrepreneurial spirit and drive.
>
> Nick: Yeah, it's almost like it's blind courage, in a sense, where nothing that's in our way is anything that we feel is bad enough or tough enough to stop us. That's how we've looked at it from the very beginning. No matter what, we're going to be successful and we're going to do every single thing that we can to ensure that our dream becomes a reality.
>
> If you're going to be successful, something just clicks inside of you like this primal instinct and you're like, "You know what? I have to do this. I have to be this aggressive and this hardworking to make this product work."

You must beat back negative thoughts and feelings and, just like Nick and Elyse said, forge ahead aggressively and work hard in the face of such resistance… and that takes **Guts**.

The Takeaway

If you don't have the **Guts** to face your own fears and set goals that your heart desires, then you will never ever take the first step towards reaching them.

Sometimes, it takes a shitload of courage to step out of your comfort zone and start the ball rolling toward making major changes in your life and the world around you. The bigger your goals, the scarier it can be.

But if you don't have that initial courage then you will continue to sit in your comfy place and bitch and moan about everything while others step over your whining ass to get the job done.

However, if you want to be a contributor to making changes, both in your life and the world around you, you've got to get off your ass and turn your energy toward making achievements that lead to success.

Before you can even start the quest for success, you have to slay the beasts of negativity... and you do that through **Guts**!

NOTE

Guts is really about the willingness to accept the fact that you may fail and the ability to push yourself beyond what is comfortable.

– Dr. Kevin Kruger – President of NASPA: Student Affairs Administrators in Higher Education

Chapter 6

GUTS IS NOT THE ABSENCE OF FEAR

Bravery is being the only one who knows you're afraid.

Franklin P. Jones - reporter, public relations executive, humorist

In our quest for understanding and acquiring G.R.I.T., we've seen that my entire mindset is built on the foundation of **Guts** and that equals courage to face our fears and forge ahead, even in our darkest hours.

However, does having courage mean that we do not have fear? Fuck no! Everyone fears something or has fear arise at some point. Even those men and women standing directly in the line of fire of whatever threat looms before them experience fear.

Being brave doesn't mean you aren't afraid. Being brave means that you control your fears instead of them controlling you. You swallow hard, take a deep breath and rush headlong into the fray of battle. **That's** how victories are won, both on the battle field and in the business world.

If you're going to make a difference and see your dreams fulfilled, you're going to need to grab your fears by the tail and fling them out of your way. Forging ahead into the unknown is scary and you are most certainly going to face fears. But you don't let those fuckers control you. No. You stare them down, knock them out of the way and continue on your way toward success.

NOTE

> Without bravery, you will have no success. Execution is for the brave only. Guts is knowing what you need to do, knowing it will hurt, and doing it anyway for positive results.
>
> But unsuccessful people won't even try. They shy away from that extra push. They are satisfied with where they are... and that satisfaction will eventually fail them.
>
> ***– Omar Tyree – Novelist***

Obstacles cannot stop you if you have the courage to face them. You might have to engage in a bitter fight, or you may have to adjust and find a way around.

But you most certainly can and will get past those obstacles and those fears if you have the **Guts** to forge ahead.

Guts Can Be Learned, but It Can't Be Taught

A lot of people believe that **Guts** is something you either have or don't have... as if it comes from birth.

Some of you might be sniveling, "But I don't have courage!" You know what? That's okay because I've got some really good news for you... courage can be learned.

Being courageous is a habit and, like with all habits, they are learned and strengthened by repeated use. We have already seen that fear is the greatest enemy to success, and we've seen that bad thoughts and feelings can thwart progress.

Therefore, in order to increase your courage... the courage needed to overcome obstacles and reach your goals... you need to consistently face your fears, take control of your negative thoughts and emotions, and go out there on a daily basis and not let anything get in your fucking way.

Of course, you may stumble, tumble and fall the first few times out, but if you learn from your mistakes, get back into the saddle and try again, that process will eventually become a habit... and a damned good habit at that!

NOTE

A lot of times, people aren't willing to even take risks. But if you don't have the guts, the courage and the bravery then you won't even step out and try.

If you don't have that courage and bravery in the beginning, you won't ever experience

> those wonderful things that can come from taking risks.
>
> *– Crystal Paine – Founder of MoneySavingMom.com*

Syndicated advice columnist Ann Landers obviously knew this principle well. She wrote:

"If I were asked to give what I considered the single most useful bit of advice for all humanity, it would be this: Expect trouble as an inevitable part of life and, when it comes, hold your head high. Look it squarely in the eye and say, 'I will be bigger than you. You cannot defeat me.'"

That's a great piece of advice for achieving success.

During my interview with Paul LeJoy, we discussed how he acquired the **Guts** to overcome seemingly insurmountable odds to become the success he is today from that of a poor beginning in Cameroon, Africa.

Paul replied:

> I had no other choice. Come on, man! I had no choice because life is full of adversity. How do you survive those adversities? You have to have the guts, you must be brave, you must be strong, you must be bold.
>
> How did I get the guts? Because of these adversities in life. And not just my own, but from other people around me that need my help because they're helpless

> themselves. It's not just about me. It's also about others that I can help. It's about my little world that God put me in. How can I make a difference? That's how I got my guts.

Paul wasn't born with courage to overcome extreme poverty and oppression. He acquired his **Guts** through the tests, trials and adversities that arose in his life.

But instead of cowering into his comfort zone where he was expected to stay, he exercised the courage to face the challenges and overcome his situation as well as help those struggling around him.

A hell of a lot of people are born into similar situations as Paul and a greater number of people have it a lot fucking easier than him. Yet these people never take the steps to do anything about it.

If you want to break free from your circumstances and soar into the skies of success, you have to muster up the courage... the **Guts**... to take the necessary risks to make that transition.

TWO CENTS' WORTH

> No matter what kind of difficulties and pressures you face, you need to have the courage to dare and challenge difficulties with determination. This is one prerequisite for success.
>
> *– Li Gang – CEO of DloDlo*

The Fear of Taking Risks

All fears over taking risks have a common root... loss.

People fear losing money, fear losing property, fear losing popularity, fear losing their reputation, fear losing loved ones, fear losing work, fear losing their life, etc. And the thing about achieving goals that lead to a successful life is that every damned one of them involves risk of some kind. Nobody on the face of this fucking planet has ever gained anything that is of any value without taking or facing some kind of risk.

Why? Because pursuing and fulfilling dreams encompasses the need to step out into the unknown where those pesky fears live.

If you think about it, life in general is one big assed risk. When you get up in the morning and jump in your car, you are risking having a debilitating accident on the way to work. Once you get to work, you run the risk of encountering a moody boss and getting fired.

Hell, just by sticking that fucking piece of fatty steak or sugary cake in your pie hole, you are running the risk of having a heart attack or stroke! The point is... risks are everywhere!

If you're going to fear taking risks, then you had better just pull the damned blankets over your head when the alarm goes off and stay in bed all day. Of course, even if you did that, you would be running the risk of going insane!

The reason you don't fear jumping in your car and heading out into the helter-skelter world everyday is because doing so has become a habit of courage. You don't fear the drive and going to work. And even if you were to think of the negative possibilities,

I'll bet that you also feel deep down inside that "It will NOT happen to me!"

You have consistently practiced facing that fear to the point that it no longer controls you, but you control it instead.

TRUISM

I actually encourage people to take risks, make mistakes and experience failure because I actually believe that it is all a part of ultimate success.

To be honest, if you're playing it too safe and you never fail then your successes will be small to non-existent. That's why I talk about the bounce-back factor so when you make a mistake, you know how to correct it and turn it into a success.

– Suzanne Smith - Founder of Social Impact Architects

Take the Leap

If you don't get in your car and go to work because of the fear of losing something then you will never get there and, subsequently, never make any money. But in order to live, you have to get up, jump in the car and head to your job.

So, you've trained yourself to have courage and not fear the risks of doing so. It doesn't mean the fear of having an accident on the way isn't there, but you have learned to control that fear so that it does not affect your goals of providing a livelihood.

There is absolutely no difference in this example and taking the step to start your own business, or make your first million dollars, or produce the best product or service in a certain industry.

The only thing lacking in the process of turning these goals into common and everyday practices like jumping in your car and driving to work every day is to grab control of your fears and press ahead to the "job" of success.

If you understand the fact that everything in life comes at some degree of risk, then you can mentally prepare yourself for the challenges before you. Choose your goals, take steps towards them and make progress.

Bonnie Kanner, Founder of Shooting Star Entertainment, sums it up nicely by saying:

> We are going to, at times, have to confront defeat. In my experience, I've generally found that defeat is a temporary phase. Defeat is seldom the end of the journey. It's usually the beginning of a learned process.
>
> So, typically when I find myself up against something that other people might call a brick wall, I call it a hurdle, I

always look for the silver lining. It's all a part of the journey of preparing for what's ahead.

As an entrepreneur, we can never turn our back on something because we are afraid. Of course, I experience fear. We are always scared of being criticized, or for presenting an idea or concept or product that no one has ever done before. It is so easy to get wrapped up in other people's criticism of our project or idea and, if we did that, we would never achieve anything.

Life's One Big Fucking Gamble

We can also consider the analogy of playing poker to illustrate the path to success. You sit down at a table with other folks with the intention of making a profit off of a bet and subsequent actions. You are not going to win a damned thing if you don't make the bet.

Could you lose something by taking such risks? Quite possibly and even probably, but if you don't place the bet then I can fucking guarantee that you won't win a damned thing.

Hell, if you honestly look at it, even buying stock in a company on Wall Street is just one big fucking casino bet. Every single day, folks take the gamble that a stock that they buy today at one price will eventually increase in value and provide them with a greater price... or profit.

Now, you can up the odds of your winning by studying, learning and seeking advice, just like you can in poker. And you should know well that Wall Street isn't a guaranteed gold mine because a ton of people have lost their asses (myself included) when sudden shifts in the market occur for whatever reason.

Investment in companies, currencies, commodities, properties and other markets and items carries the exact same risk as gambling at the local casino, only the stakes are often far greater.

Yet folks take those risks on a daily basis without batting an eye. Why? Because they have created the habit of courageously doing so by rejecting the fears of possible loss and forging ahead to prosperity.

Now, the more knowledge you acquire and the more you hone your skills, the greater the percentage of success, but it all involves risk.

I'm showing you in this book how you can up the odds of success by developing the skills of G.R.I.T.

The Takeaway

Life is all about risks. It's how you handle life that decides whether or not you simply chug along the best you can by exerting the minimum amount of effort and facing the minimum amount of risk, or you make the gambles and take the risks of becoming something more than ordinary.

When it boils down to it, what you get out of life is directly related to what you put into it. People that whine and complain about the situation they're in have no one to blame but themselves.

YOU have the power to change your life.

YOU have the power to become a success.

YOU have the power to change the lives of others and the world around you.

The bottom line is... if you never take the leap because you are afraid of losing something then you will never gain anything.

However, if you're ready to crawl out of your comfort zone and start making things happen then have the **Guts** to do it... and the next step is turning the page.

TRUISM

The bravery to step out, to believe in yourself, to have faith in your abilities is everything.

It's the people who walk in fear that live smaller lives. There's no doubt about that. I was surrounded by very small thinkers, meaning people who believed that happiness was a 9 to 5 job, a steady paycheck, two week's vacation... that happiness was a routine formula.

I never subscribed to that. For me, life and happiness were about shaking all that up and creating your own formula and having the guts to believe you could step out on your own. You didn't have to depend on an employer, or a husband, or someone else to make your financial success or make your life happy.

– Andy Paige - Beauty and Style Expert, TV Personality, Entrepreneur and Author of the bestseller Style on a Shoestring

03

R is for Resilience

Chapter 7

THE FOUR TRAITS OF RESILIENCE

"I think that it (resilience) is crucial. In fact, I would question one's ability to be successful without a strong sense of resilience."

Andy Thompson – Pastor of World Overcomers Christian Church

The next ingredient of the G.R.I.T. way of thinking is **Resilience**.

What the fuck exactly is that? Well, I'm glad you asked.

Resilience is the ability to adapt to various pressures, stresses, threats, traumas and other adverse events and conditions of life. They can be physical, mental, or emotional tests and **Resilience** is what gets you through such hard times.

Andy Thompson's quote at the beginning of this chapter shows how important he believes that this trait is to the process of success.

Andy went on to say during our interview:

> I believe resilience is the drive that motivates us to push through situations or circumstances that would cause most people to give up or quit.

> Resilience is an active factor that separates those who are willing to overcome the hardships of life because they see the good things to come in the distance.
>
> Everyone is subject to hardships. It is a part of life. Some people feel weighed down and burdened by them and others feel empowered to grow from them.
>
> It is a practice of perspective.

Did you catch what Andy said? There are two powerful points that he made in that one short paragraph.

First of all, you're going to get knocked the fuck down on more than one occasion as you journey through life. That's a simple fact that every human on the planet can bet on. If you can't keep plugging ahead in the face of the defeats, pitfalls and failures that pop up then you just are not going to make much progress towards your goals.

Secondly, Andy points out that **Resilience** is a matter of perspective. This is an important one. Some people have this trait deeply ingrained in them from the get-go and the "others" trudge through life thinking they just don't have the "stuff" to overcome harsh obstacles. They see the pain and suffering... the risk... as being just too much to bear and they settle into their shitty, comfy spot.

Does having resilience mean you're not going to experience pain and suffering?

Fuck no! As a matter of fact, people tend to develop stronger **Resilience** when they go through bad experiences because they are forced to keep going despite difficult and often seemingly insurmountable odds.

The **Resilience** to get your ass up off the floor and press ahead helps strengthen your G.R.I.T.!

TWO CENTS' WORTH

When you love what you do and your purpose serves humanity's greater well-being, your drive becomes your passion and any difficulties you face as an individual or team simply become another hurdle to leap.

Each time we leap through, our legs get stronger.

– Li Gang – CEO of DloDlo

Resilience contains four major traits that can be honed and developed through thoughts, actions and increasingly positive behaviors. Yes, this characteristic can be learned and honed, so you have no fucking excuse to continue sitting on your ass feeling sorry for yourself!

When you make the decision to focus on and strengthen these traits, your **Resilience** AND your overall G.R.I.T. will increase as well!

Trait One: *Recovery*

The very foundational core of **Resilience** is the ability to recover. Recover from what? From change, setbacks and failures that occur throughout life.

In order to maximize your potential, improve the quality of your life and reach your goals on the road to success, you've got to get up when you've been knocked down and continue pressing forward.

It's like going to work even though you have the flu and feel horrible. You've got responsibilities to attend to and a paycheck to make so you get the fuck up when you would rather stay home and you go.

Now, some battles of life can be ferocious and taxing. They can severely kick your ass and cause physical, mental, emotional and financial wounds. I personally know about this one because I was diagnosed with cancer. But instead of falling into a pattern of whining and crying about it, I made the decision to pick myself up and do what I had to do to find a solution.

TRUISM

You can get all of the degrees in the world, but they won't teach you these types of skills. I don't think a person knows their true strength or what they're really made of until they hit rock bottom. It's then that you decide to give up or push forward.

Since launching my company, I've hit rock bottom

> multiple times. Cancer, financial losses and even deceit almost derailed my journey multiple times. Thankfully, my vision meant everything to me and no amount of heartache was going to stop me.
>
> ***– Tiffany Krumins – Entrepreneur and Creator of Ava the Elephant® talking medicine dispensers for children***

The principles are the same. I had responsibilities to meet and a paycheck to earn. But more importantly, I am NOT going to let cancer or anything or anyone else kick my ass! So I implemented **Resilience** and I fucking pushed my way through the battles and dark times until I won the victory.

Roxi Bahar Hewertson, CEO of Highland Consulting Group, has spent more than 35 years gleaning truths about what makes all types of leaders do the things they do, both the successful and not so successful.

When I asked Roxi what her take was on **Resilience** and the role it plays in leadership, she responded:

> I define it (resilience) as the ability to cope dynamically with stress and adversity and to "bounce back". It is a process that allows us to build "muscle memory". I think it's a lot like an inoculation that helps the body reject infection.

> It is critical to one's success in life, not, in my opinion, one's potential for success. We all face adversity in many, many ways throughout our lives and we ALL bounce back to some extent or we'd die.

The differentiator for those who are successful and those who are just getting by or not getting by always has that person's resilience level in the equation.

This "process" of "bouncing back" can be summed up as recovery. Just like healing from a sickness takes time before you regain full health, getting the shit knocked out of you through various events of life also requires a period of recovery… a time to "lick your wounds", so to speak.

And, just as a sickness works to strengthen the body's resistance to the source of the attack, what is learned from bad experiences also works to increase our resistance and **Resilience** against the same situations, circumstances and stupid decisions that got us there in the first place.

We tuck those lessons away in the back recesses of our mind, strengthening our "muscle memory", as Roxi puts it.

Trait Two: *Learning*

John Dewey, the famous American psychologist, educational reformer and philosopher, said:

"Failure is instructive. The Person who really thinks learns quite as much from his failures as from his successes."

This is an absolute foundational principle for advancing in life. If you don't fucking learn from your mistakes then you are doomed to not only repeat them, but to remain in some low or mediocre place where you do nothing except bang your head against a wall.

People like to throw the phrase around that "ignorance is bliss", but I'm here to tell you that ignorance is also the food of persistent failures.

When you learn from life's experiences, you arm yourself with knowledge that feeds **Resilience**. You don't only get up and progress because you've got courage, but you now add to that the wisdom of gleaned knowledge.

You're not only meaner, but you're now smarter and wiser!

Trait Three: *Caution*

When you get the shit kicked out of you by some life event and you learn the lessons of that beating, you will also develop another characteristic that will boost your **Resilience**... caution.

Now, a part of G.R.I.T. is having Guts, but it is at the beginning for a good reason. Guts will help you overcome your doubts and fears, and get the success ball rolling, but it will take the qualities of **Resilience** to keep the momentum going.

Once you recover and acknowledge the lessons that come from it, you need to then take that experience and knowledge and move along your path with a bit more caution.

That doesn't mean become a chicken-shit and retreat from adversity! No. You take a bit more caution about HOW you apply the knowledge and experience that you have acquired.

It is said that doing the same thing over and over again while getting the same results is the definition of insanity. I'm not talking about being fucking insane. I'm talking about having the G.R.I.T. to become as successful as you'd like to be.

Taking what you've gleaned from your experiences and being cautious during future endeavors will help increase your **Resilience** and ensure your continued success.

Trait Four: *Endurance*

There is one quality of resilience that is born out of repeated attempts at advancing in life... endurance.

Getting knocked down, rising back up, learning from your mistakes and proceeding with more caution creates endurance deep inside of you that you can and will get over the next mountain and the next and the next until you reach your goal.

The more you get your ass up and try again, the more you learn about what the fuck you can do. As you figure your talents out and develop your skills, you learn to endure and become more confident in yourself and your abilities.

When you have endurance, you can fight harder, act bolder. Those without, believe deep down that they can win or they wouldn't fucking fight at all!

The more times you fail and rise back up, the more endurance you build so that you can overcome any other challenges that may come your way.

The second part of G.R.I.T., therefore, is **Resilience** which is the ability to keep on pressing forward even when you've been hit hard.

NOTE

Resilience is an ability within the mind to move one's self through feelings of defeat. It says, "Something way better is beyond this and I'm now one step closer to experiencing it".

– September Dohrmann – COO of CEO Space

Chapter 8

THE ART OF NOT GIVING UP

You can't be a pioneer if you are willing to settle.

Rebecca Rescate - Founder of CitiKitty & Rebecca Rescate Inc. & Co-Founder of HoodiePillow

As we have seen, it takes **Guts** to survive, but it takes another piece of G.R.I.T. to bounce back. You have to have **Resilience** to get up and move on after everyone else has dropped out.

Many people fail simply because they don't stay in the game. Success comes from weathering the storm when everybody else has been swept away.

May 3rd is when I celebrate my birthday. It wasn't the day I was conceived, but the day I learned I had cancer. I'll never forget that day (the memory forever etched into the back of my mind). I went to bed healthy and woke up the following morning thinking I was going to die. Soon afterwards, I escaped death and realized I was one lucky bastard and that moving forward I needed to live life not just exist. Cancer absolutely has a way of changing people; it fucking changed me forever.

> There's a lot of pressure on you as a person as an entrepreneur. Not everybody is meant to be an entrepreneur and not everybody is cut out for it.
>
> In fact, a lot of people shouldn't be doing it because they don't have resilience. They can't weather those storms that are going to come against them.
>
> You've got to have resilience to succeed.
>
> ***– Dan Caldwell – Entrepreneur and Co-Founder of TapouT sports clothing***

Ever since this life-changing event, I have become this creative creature and collector of quotes and I have created a commemorative jersey out of them. Some of my main quotes are:

> *"When something bad happens, you have three choices; you can let it define you, let it destroy you, or you can let it strengthen you."*
>
> *"It is hard to beat a person who never gives up."*
>
> *"Do not give up! The beginning is the hardest part."*

And most importantly:

> *"No one ever drowned in sweat."*

These quotes have become etched in my subconscious and I live by them. They have come from the refining fires of **Resilience** that lies inside and that have helped me through some of my darkest hours.

Billy Mann, former Chief Creative Officer, President of New Music A&R, and President of Global Artist Management for EMI, describes **Resilience** by drawing a reference from the movie *Rocky* and paralleling it to professional life:

> Like a lot of Philadelphians of my generation, I am obsessed with Rocky Balboa because it's not what happens in the ring that makes him a champion; it's his resilience. It's about getting back up even after you've been hit by what appears to be the stronger challenger, the bigger, the taller, the better funded, the more connected, the glitzy, and the crowd favorite.
>
> I often tell people in the music business that if you want to be "right" 90% of the time, (about a song, a production, an artist, a product, a platform), just saying whatever is put forth won't work and you will have an incredibly high strike rate. For most songwriters, being rejected is 90% of their life, and having resilience is merely the cover charge at your point of entry. But I will say, "getting back up", in and of itself, is not resilience.
>
> Resilience requires a commitment to a destination: a dream, a purpose, a predetermined outcome free of material goals, but clear on life goals.

What Billy is sharing here is that following your own inner guidance is a big part of **Resilience.**

In most of the arenas of life, if you get knocked down and decide to stay down because you're afraid, uncomfortable, intimidated, have your feelings hurt, or whatever feeble feeling you're having at the time then you are not going to make any progress, much less succeed. You've got to pick your sore and humiliated ass up off the floor and try again!

Chester Elton of The Culture Works goes even further. He says that **Resilience** is not only about coming back, it's about:

"Being able to fail and leave it in the past, and move on quickly."

He draws particular attention to letting go of the negative:

> It's not easy. We tend to be hard-wired to be negative. It's sort of a protective mechanism. It tells us where danger is, you know. And so, I think when we fail, we tend to dwell in it.
>
> I know early in my career, that was a real issue for me. It was really hard to let things go. I really admire entrepreneurs, in particular, that have that resilience. They have a great idea, they try it out, it fails, they fail quick, they move on to the next great idea, and I have great admiration for people that have that kind of resilience. It's like they say, "It's not really how you start or where you are halfway through. It's how you finish."

> And I think that people that are resilient find that extra gear to really finish, whether it's finish up and move on, or push to the end. When you think about the alternative, which is where most people end where you dwell on that negativity, it's such a huge waste of time and energy, and you're unhappy and you make everybody around you unhappy. Therefore, that idea of being resilient and moving on is such a wonderful principle.

You have to keep coming back without limiting yourself to what's immediately doable. Instead ask yourself, "What's possible?"

If you give in to the negativity of harsh and seemingly defeating experiences then you significantly limit your ability to overcome, both for that particular instance and those that follow.

TRUISM

> I would describe resilience as the ability to fight through anything that's a challenge to you, and you pursue it with vengeance and you pursue it at the highest level.
>
> That's my definition of it. It's nothing elaborate, nothing profound. I just think that when you put your heart and soul and mind into something and you are

> able to follow through and stick to it and not give up... you've got to be resilient to do this.
>
> ***– Marc Williams – Founder and CEO of Williams Communications***

Stumbling, bumbling and falling are inevitable parts of the journey. The trick is to not only get back up, but learn from those experiences and move on. You can bet your ass there's another obstacle around the next bend and you can equally be sure that it will be different than the last. So, there's no sense dwelling on past mistakes. Get back up, learn from the experience and move on.

Bev Vines-Haines and Charlotte Clary are two mothers and grandmothers who combined their knowledge a decade ago about herbal remedies and started their own all-natural salve business. As time went by, they wanted to give all their children and grandchildren (they have nearly 40 between them) healthy candy which led to their launching Ice Chips candy company in 2009.

Was the process an easy one? We discussed that and they said:

> Charlotte: One time, Bev and I were speaking to about 500 people and I was asked the question at the end, "How did you deal with all that failure?" The reason they asked that is because Bev and I have started 30 different companies between us, some together and some separately.

When I was asked that question, it kind of took me back. I answered and said, "Huh! That's funny. I have never ever considered any of those things failures!"

What we did was we learned a new skill in each one of those businesses. We learned something beneficial from each one of the businesses, so we took what we learned, and we built on it. That is the definition of our resilience.

Bev: I would say we're pretty conservative and we're very brave. So, I think that when we started out, we did not stop and consider the economy or other obstacles. We just thought we had a great idea and we would just make the product. When it comes to Ice Chips candy, when we formulated that, we knew within a week that we had a once-in-a-lifetime product.

Bev and Charlotte's experience is a common one in the ranks of the successful. We don't focus on the obstacles, but on the vision. And when hard times come knocking, we fucking keep pressing on until the victory comes... even if it takes 30 failed businesses to get there.

TRUISM

Resilience is the ability to continue chasing your passion even after continued heartbreak and letdown. It's a strength that can't be described and can't be stopped. It means knowing that

> your end goal is worth more to you than the pain you may have to endure to get there.
>
> *– Tiffany Krumins - Entrepreneur and Creator of Ava the Elephant® talking medicine dispensers for children*

The Takeaway

Resilience is about the staying power needed to keep you in the fight until the victory is won by helping you recover, learn valuable lessons, proceed with caution and become more confident that you can both make it to your goal and overcome any son-of-a-bitch that might stand in your way.

Staying focused on the goal is a good way to strengthen Resilience. Pastor Andy Thompson likes to rely on the Bible to help him achieve that. He says:

> Joshua 1:9 says, "Be strong and courageous. Do not be frightened, and do not be dismayed". Resilience is a result of strength and perseverance, and this verse helps me stay reminded of that.

When it comes down to making progress towards your success goals, you need to be strong and persevere.

In western civilizations, imperfections are largely viewed as things that should be tucked away and hidden out of sight. Many people therefore are mentally and emotionally handicapped from the get-go, either avoiding taking the risks that might reveal their imperfections or spending most of their time and effort trying to camouflage those shortcomings. A perfect example of this lies in Andy Paige's story in chapter 3 where she took on a suffocating amount of debt to acquire higher education just to hide her "imperfection" of being a high school dropout from a rural part of Alabama.

While talking with Business Development Psychologist and Culture Architect Dr. David Gruder, he brought up a very interesting perspective on this topic from an Eastern culture. He said:

> I would describe resilience as the ability to turn the unexpected twists and turns in the road into opportunities and blessings, even when they're unasked for and even undesired.
>
> There's a worldview in Japan called wabi-sabi. It doesn't really have a parallel in the Western world, but it's essentially a worldview that sees the beauty in imperfection and emphasizes it. The classic version or image associated with wabi-sabi is when you put a piece of pottery into a kiln to be fired and it comes out cracked. Instead of throwing it away, you fill in the crack with gold or gold-colored paint in order to emphasize or symbolize the process of finding the beauty in the imperfection.
>
> To me, that's resilience.

In a sense, that is exactly what all people of success are. We have gone through the fire and have been cracked and sometimes broken. But instead of chucking our attempts at success in the shitter, we fill those imperfections with the gold of knowledge, wisdom and experience.

Successful people appear to be beautiful works of art to those admiring them from a distance, but it sure as hell isn't because we don't have cracks! We just choose to fill those fuckers in with gold and keep moving forward.

The point is, if you spend your time worrying about your imperfections and shortcomings then you will never get a damned thing done. Stop whining and crying about your weaknesses, apply some **Resilience** and get the fuck out there and earn your cracks!

TWO CENTS' WORTH

Resilience is being able to learn from whatever it is that happens. Then take your learning and go and build off of that and do something different or better the next time around.

– Stacey Ferreira – Entrepreneur, Speaker, Author and Co-Founder of MySocialCloud and Co-Founder and CEO of Forrge

Chapter 9

SUCCESS IS ALWAYS JUST AROUND THE CORNER

You were born to win. But to be a winner, you must plan to win, prepare to win and expect to win.

Zig Ziglar – salesman, author, motivational speaker

Mr. Ziglar hit the nail on the head. He knew that every person has the ability to be a success. It's the exact same message I'm passing on to you in this book only with a different twist.

Every single person has the ability to muster up, develop and utilize G.R.I.T. to reach their goals.

However, to actually achieve success, you have to plan on it, prepare for it and fucking go out and get it!

The journey can often be long with success seemingly never manifesting. It can feel like success is always just around the next corner, but when you turn that corner, it's once again just out of reach.

Let me tell you something that I've learned from experience. If you keep chasing success, there truly is nothing able to prevent you from attaining it.

The secret is to get up every damned day, put the events of the previous day behind you and get back out there. That, my friends, is called **Resilience**.

Mr. Ziglar expressed this simple truth when he said:

"Yesterday ended last night. Today is a brand new day."

It can be fucking hard to get up and face another day, especially when the battles of life are raging. But if you don't get back out there, day after fucking day, you will never catch up with success.

NOTE

Resilience is the ability to cope with rejection and disappointment when plans don't work, when inevitable mistakes happen and when you have an unexpected set-back which requires a re-gathering of self-determination, a bit of re-thinking, re-planning and determination to try, try and try again.

Resilience is a component of the fact that there is no such word as "can't".

– Lara Morgan – Entrepreneur and Founder of CompanyShortcuts.com

Keep Moving Forward

Although some people consider it to be elusive, it's not a bad thing to see success as lying just around the next corner. That attitude keeps you pressing forward until you reach your goals.

The focus, therefore, shouldn't be on the allusiveness of success or you may end up saying "fuck it!" Instead, the focus should be on pressing ahead through the thick and thin, the good and bad, the feasts and famines until you eventually reach your destination.

During my interview with Roxi Bahar Hewertson, CEO of Highland Consulting Group, she touched on this very principle.

She said:

> Keep moving forward. Even small accomplishments and gains need to be recognized as positive steps of progress. These enable you to move toward your goals.
>
> Instead of focusing on tasks that seem unachievable, ask yourself, "What's one thing I know I can accomplish today that helps me move in the direction I want to go?"

Too many folks increase their own stress, weaken their own sanity and produce their own defeat by trying to do too much too fast.

In doing so, these same people tend to get bogged down with the thoughts and feelings of never reaching their destination. Their goals never seem to materialize and always seem to lie just around the next corner. "What the fuck?" they say, "I'm never going to get there." So they quit.

However, if you recognize and acknowledge every little step as a victory that propels you towards your goal then the success that lies ahead will appear within reach. "I just need to take another step," you say, and so you fucking do.

It's like our earlier example of going to work. If you focused on all the possible and existing dangers that lie along the way to and from your job, you would never arrive, if you ever took the first fucking step at all.

However, if you simply focused on the first step and then the next leg of the journey and the next and so on, and applied your energy and resources to achieving those small goals, you would one day wake up and find yourself discovering places very few have seen.

Your Guts would cause you to face the task and take that first step. But it is your **Resilience** that would carry you through all the obstacles and setbacks to finally arrive at your destination.

TWO CENTS' WORTH

When you come up against some kind of challenge that is difficult, that strains your resources, and you are able to deal with those challenges, cope with them and grow from them, I think this is what resilience really means.

–Dr. Harold Koenig – Physician, Director of the Center for Spirituality, Theology and Health at Duke University Medical Center and Author of over 40 books

Aim at Manageable Goals

It is absolutely necessary to have big, lofty goals. If you never believe that you will own your own business than you will never have one. If you never see yourself as the President of the United States than you will never fill those shoes.

The reason you will never reach such goals is not because you aren't necessarily capable or qualified. The reason is that if you don't have those goals in mind to start with then you will not take the steps and learn the lessons along the way to effectively reach those goals.

Another smart quote from Zig Ziglar is:

"If you aim at nothing, you'll hit it every time."

Pretty fucking clear cut piece of advice. If you don't have goals than you will never... ever... reach them because, well, they don't fucking exist!

Now, on the other side of the coin, you can't do epic shit without setting smaller, achievable goals. You can want a multi-million-dollar business all you want, but if you don't set short-term steps to get there then you'll fail miserably... and that's a fact.

Having the **Resilience** to creatively meet, alter and manage change in life was brought up by Dr. Kevin Kruger, President of NASPA - Student Affairs Administrators in Higher Education. He said:

> I think resilience is the ability to meet and embrace life's challenges and to be able to develop strategies to overcome those challenges or develop new learning about yourself and others as a result of those challenges. The goal is to not get mired in self-pity or depression, or to lack the ability to motivate yourself when you face those kinds of challenges.
>
> Creativity is a big part of that formula. I think that you can learn through resilience about how to deal with problems, make new approaches and become creative about how you might approach something – a similar challenge – the next time, and not assume that a similar set of challenges will always be there. Instead, you have to think that there may be ways to overcome

> those challenges and take a more creative and innovative approach to the same set of problems.

It's like playing football. You don't start at your own 10-yard line and throw a "hail Mary" for a touchdown 90 yards down the field. That type of action is reserved for desperate situations at the end of the game when time is running out because it rarely ever works.

No. You get down and fucking dig, push and charge for a few yards at a time until your main goal is within striking distance.

We can also use the analogy of reaching an office on the top floor of a skyscraper. You need an effective plan of action because twinkling your nose like a fucking fairy won't get you up there.

Now, the surest plan is to take the elevator which will get you there faster, but you run the risk that it may stop working and leave you stranded for hours. Another plan could be to take the stairs which could give you a fucking heart attack if you're heading to the 89th floor, but it can be done with a good deal of **Resilience**.

If you've got a whole lot of G.R.I.T., you might choose to jump out of a fucking plane and parachute to the top of the building. That would definitely get you there faster than anything else, but it also comes with a shitload of extra risks. Your chute might not open, the wind might blow you off course and slam you into another building, you might land in the ceiling fan and be chewed to bits, or you might get arrested and spend some time in jail.

The point is that you have to first have a big goal, like making a touchdown or reaching that top floor office, and then you have to plan a series of manageable goals to achieve the pinnacle of success.

It's up to you how much risk you put into the effort. The greater the risk, the faster your chances of reaching your destination, but it also increases the severity of any failures.

Now, let's move on to the third aspect of the G.R.I.T. mindset that helps achieve success.

04

I is for Initiative

Chapter 10

THE FOUR TRAITS OF INITIATIVE

Without initiative, leaders are simply workers in leadership positions.

Robert "Bo" Bennett, American businessman

The next element of the G.R.I.T. mindset that is necessary for achieving success is **Initiative** which is defined as the ability to assess and initiate things independently.

It's all well and good to have the Guts to face your fears and get things moving and the Resilience to rise up from defeats and keep moving. But you also need the drive and desire to take control of the reins and get the job done YOURSELF.

You can't really learn the quality of **Initiative** because the drive to succeed comes from within.

With that said, you can absolutely learn and hone the traits of **Initiative** which will strengthen this asset and make it work better for you. And you can also get help along the way which is great and often quite welcome.

However, other people are NOT going to make you a success if you don't apply yourself. You have to fucking do that yourself and you get it done with **Initiative**.

Bo Bennett is a successful businessman and he knows about **Initiative** which is obvious from the opening quote.

Bo and I have a lot in common. We both have a ton of G.R.I.T. and the **Initiative** contained therein.

People like us... people with G.R.I.T.... we see problems and things that need to be changed and we take the **Initiative** to tackle them and get them done!

Jim Schroer is another go-getter success story. Jim is a marketing innovator with over three decades of experience and currently is Principal of The New England Consulting Group, Inc.

Jim told me:

> When you need to change, if something needs to change for the better, or if you need to fix something that went wrong, that's when the quality of initiative is really, really, really necessary. It is 100 times harder to change something for the better than it is to just keep it going the same way.
>
> I think that's why we don't have a lot of good leaders that can initiate change. Most of the time, companies want people to maintain the status quo. When we need something to change, we need qualities like initiative and those aren't easy to find in leaders today.

The corporate world today is a fucking mess because they have strayed away en masse from people with G.R.I.T. Instead, those running the companies and corporations have turned to hiring and promoting fancy pants employees with designer degrees to stick in leadership roles based almost solely on their time spent at college and their skills for bullshitting.

Those with G.R.I.T. are not only often better equipped to make their mark on the world, but they usually have admirable qualities that stand the tests of time as well as bring real, lasting success. Therefore, let's focus on identifying, understanding and developing the traits that give G.R.I.T. its teeth by continuing with **Initiative**.

Trait One: *Improvisation*

The power of improvisation is a foundational pillar of **Initiative**.

You absolutely must have the ability to improvise and go off script in the business world as well as life in general.

If you have any years under your belt at all then you know damned well that a whole host of unexpected shit can pop up without a moment's notice.

If you aren't able to make immediate adjustments, those unexpected wrenches thrown in the works can fuck up your plans and severely delay, if not destroy, your goals.

I was in the Marine Corps and I can tell you that being able to improvise was a key fucking element driven deep into your psyche.

Why? Because if you were called to the battlefield where you are surrounded by other people hell bent on killing you and things go off script, you have to make improvisations... and you have to make them fucking NOW or you die!

The business world may not be quite so extreme, but the same principle applies. When you are moving along according to plan and something unexpected arises, if you don't improvise and make instant adjustments then you can lose millions of dollars in potential business.

Not being able to improvise in such situations can mean the death of your company or other long-term plans. That can be damned near as bad as dying physically!

Trait Two: *Intuition*

Have you ever had a nagging feeling down inside your gut that told you something was either right or wrong even though everyone and everything else on the outside was screaming for or against it?

Well, that "gut feeling" is intuition and it is another foundational pillar of **Initiative**.

Folks that grab the bull by the horns and make things happen generally have an uncanny sense of intuition. This gut feeling nudges them to make decisions for or against something even when all the voices and signs are screaming to the contrary. Hell, a large part of having Guts stems from this base sense!

The very meaning of intuition is having the ability to instinctively understand present trends, moods and environments without having to process data through the reasoning process of your gourd.

Many a person has risen to success, wealth and fame by acting on the prodding of their instincts. Intuition goes beyond hearing the pounding of the drums and, instead, listens to the underlying pulse of what is really going on.

If you are going to be successful then you sometimes need to ignore the blaring world of facts, figures and reasoning and simply act on what your gut is telling you.

You will need **Initiative** to pull that off.

Trait Three: *Partnership*

Although **Initiative** encompasses the drive to strike out on your own, very few things of value in life are actually acquired without any assistance.

When talking about starting a business, you normally can't get moving without entering a partnership with a bank or other loan institution. If you want your company to grow then you will need to enter partnerships with investors and stockholders.

Hell, unless you fucking want to do every single task in your company by yourself, you need to enter into partnerships with people that are generally labeled as employees!

Times even arise when you need to be the one supplying the help to others. You enter into partnerships with other people, companies, or organizations that benefit them in order to broaden the reach of your brand, or to simply give back something that you've acquired and achieved, like knowledge, a good name, or finances.

Having G.R.I.T. means you are fucking ready, willing and able to tackle the journey and problems along the way by yourself. But it also means being smart enough to enter relationships with others that are equally beneficial to you both.

There really are no "lone wolves" in the business world.

Trait Four: *Contemplation*

Initiative sometimes requires that you make nearly instant adjustments to your goal-reaching plan.

However, it also consists of stepping back and taking a good, long look at what has transpired, what is transpiring and what could or should transpire.

Contemplation is a valuable part of the learning process and we've already taken a look at the importance that learning from mistakes and failures has in the G.R.I.T. mindset.

Lessons are not fully learned unless we contemplate them deeply and thoughtfully. By analyzing situations in this way, our conscious and subconscious are both able to explore the various elements that produced either the positive or negative results in the first place and that can make things better or worse the next time similar situations arise.

True and effective learning are born out of contemplation of the data and experiences provided.

Contemplation therefore deepens and sharpens one's **Initiative**.

Chapter 11

JUMP START TO SELF START

You are essentially who you create yourself to be and all that occurs in your life is the result of your own making.

Stephen Richards - author, investigative journalist

Initiative keeps you moving towards the goal regardless of the obstacles, criticism, or even when you feel like shit.

Guts and resilience are great, but if you don't maintain that driving desire to continue forward, you won't go far.

Initiative automatically presents the risk of failure, which is why going after your goals is well worth it. The effort either takes you forward into a new direction, or you fail and the lessons you glean from those failures take you in a new direction.

When it comes to showing **Initiative**, you don't have to look much further than Scott Gerber. He is the founder of the Young Entrepreneur Council (YEC), a sought-after public speaker, an internationally syndicated business columnist and best-selling author of *Never Get a "Real" Job: How to Dump Your Boss, Build a Business and Not Go Broke.*

Scott has this to say about **Initiative**:

> Initiative to me is an undying sense of being driven to an end goal regardless of any obstacle in your way, barrier, or otherwise, to achieve what people say you can't do or consider to be impossible. And that you, and sometimes only you, believe it to be achievable. A necessary mountain to climb would be a good way to describe it.
>
> The world as we now see it is a result of the initiative of many individuals who saw the world in a different way than what it is today, decided to take action, change it actively and execute it to the point where they saw it become a reality. I think that today initiative is a sorely lacking component of many people's worldviews.

A lot of people like to rely on "luck" as a factor in what they do and how results transpire.

However, luck is nothing but a fucking excuse and if you rely on luck to get you places then you probably will never arrive. Of course, there are times when people or events seem to appear "magically" out of thin air at just the right time, but most "luck" is a combination of a million behind-the-scenes efforts and actions that produce those seemingly magical experiences.

Scott has an interesting insight into this topic. He talks about how to get over, or around, the obstacles through **Initiative**:

> The world does not come knocking on your door anytime soon. I often like talking to people who talk about luck.

> And there is obviously a form of luck that occurs in entrepreneurship, but luck can be created.
>
> Luck is something that you can ultimately put yourself into the position where it is more attainable. You know, creating more probability in your favor for luck to occur. Luck alone doesn't get it done.
>
> The reason you are creating luck is because you are creating the initiative, because you are a self-starter. I don't think you need to wait for someone to knock on your door; you need to knock on 100 doors.
>
> You can't wait for someone to go and give you an opportunity you have to go out there and find it and take it.

R. Scott Arnell, Founding Partner of Geneva Capital, has a very precise definition of **Initiative** that more clearly demonstrates how it is used to move ideas from our minds into the very real world that surrounds us. He says:

> When I think about it, I think of initiative as the willful action by a person to move a thought or an idea from that person's inner thought world into the physical world. So, you're taking it from thoughts into reality, so to speak, and moving it into the real world where it can affect people, relationships and so forth.

> Then, when you combine those actions, or when this action's backed or underpinned by passions that are grounded in deeply held values, I really see this as initiative. It's the first step; it's the first action in moving a significant dream into reality. It's something that's an intentional action.

Actions or the lack thereof can quickly make or break you as well as tell others around you what kind of initiative you have.

NBA great, Earl "The Pearl" Monroe played for the Baltimore Bullets and the New York Knicks. He provided some insight about recognizing initiative and how having it or lacking it can "change the game".

Earl shared this account:

> There are certain times that you can clearly see breaking points in a lot of games. You can see the turnover effect of how teams are playing and how that can affect the outcome of a game.
>
> For example, in the Final Four semi-final championship game of 2014, Wisconsin was playing Kentucky and should have beaten Kentucky. But a kid came in that hadn't been playing that much. It was easy to see why because he took a shot and then he didn't hustle after the ball. I said, "Well, this is a defining moment of this game." I knew that because now the other team grabs the momentum.

> You have to be able to recognize those different points and try to seize that moment. Then the most important thing is learning how to close out games because after you seize the moment, if you don't know how to close the game out then there's no sense working that hard to get to that point.

Initiative is about taking the first step, sure. But you also have to be able to recognize opportunities, take the shots and "hustle after the ball" if you miss. Like Earl pointed out, if you don't have the drive to close out the game then all that effort applied to get to that point is wasted.

Initiative will keep you moving to fulfill your dream and help you to win the fucking game.

How bad do you WANT it?

How important is **Initiative**, which encompasses the qualities of inventiveness, ingenuity and being a self-starter, when defining one's potential for success?

I asked best-selling author, high-impact teacher and empowerment specialist, Dr. Cindy Trimm, how important **Initiative** is and this is what she had to say:

> We can always find reasons why we can't do something. There are always a thousand reasons, every single day. But a person with initiative does not ignore the obstacles, or the difficulties, but

> instead, they look beyond them and they see them as something that they prep against.
>
> To me, it's like building muscles. You can only build muscles with resistance. People who do not achieve things in life, or don't maximize their potential, are people that run away from obstacles.
>
> Success is booby-trapped; it's filled with obstacles, not to prevent you from achieving it, but to see how bad you want it.

In a nutshell, achieving your goals comes down to your desire, or how badly you want to see your dreams, ideas and thoughts come true... manifest into reality. That kind of drive will get you through a lot of CRAP!

TWO CENTS' WORTH

Initiative is about taking the first step. Without the first step, there is no journey and certainly no marathon!

Initiative is about smart thinking. It's about getting from one place to another with the least resistance.

– Bonnie Kanner – Founder of Shooting Star Entertainment

Take it from Jonny Imerman, Founder of Imerman Angels[5] which is a One-on-One Cancer Support Community, who speaks of "diving in" with **Initiative**... with everything you got:

> It's about turning away other opportunities and living another life to do WHAT you truly love, care about most, digging into your deepest passion—choosing to DIVE INTO what you love most and the change you want to see in the world!
>
> I think of it as jumping off a cliff with a blindfold and knowing that somehow, some way, you have no idea HOW, you're going to do it, but you know you're going to figure it out in the air, because you LOVE the direction that you're going in!
>
> This is true initiative!

Showing Initiative is tough. It's tough because it always requires action... sustained action. I have taken **Initiative** in

(5) Imerman Angels is the leading one-on-one cancer support community that carefully matches and individually pairs a cancer fighter or caregiver with someone who has fought and survived the same type of cancer (a Mentor Angel). These one-on-one relationships inspire hope and offer the chance to ask personal questions and receive support from someone who is uniquely familiar with the experience. The service is absolutely free and helps anyone touched by any type of cancer, at any cancer stage level, at any age, living anywhere in the world. Imerman Angels is a federally registered 501(c)(3) not-for-profit organization. www.imermanangels.org

the realm of philanthropy, but any kind of drive requires change translated into action.

I wrote an article for *Forbes* that discussed change, but in the end it was really about change resulting in action:

> No matter what your cause is, philanthropy is about change. If you see something you want to change, change it. That is the essence of being a socialpreneur. The concept of going your own way and doing your own thing shouldn't cease in the philanthropic world. The problem is, most people don't do it because it bucks tradition and goes against the grain and, frankly, it scares most people.
>
> The key is to look at each task for the opportunities they present. Sure, there may be a "perfectly fine" or traditional way of doing something to achieve a good result. But when you have a better approach or process in mind that can achieve an even more desirable outcome, it may just be time to go rogue. In today's cutthroat culture, originality is perhaps your greatest gift. Use it.

The Takeaway

When it comes to G.R.I.T., the trait of Guts will cause you to climb in a boxing ring with a big son-of-a-bitch looking to beat you to a pulp and Resilience will cause you to get back up when you're knocked down.

However, it is **Initiative** that allows you to continually and independently assess the situation during the fight and make the decisions that will keep you fighting and get you to the next round.

Initiative is a key element of G.R.I.T. that will keep you moving forward when everyone and everything else is trying to get you to move into your comfort zone. People can't make you a success.

You have to make the effort to do that yourself, with or without their help, and that takes **Initiative**.

TRUISM

> We're a small business trying to pretend we're big. We're shaking it 'til we make it here. That's our mantra.
>
> *– Nick and Elyse Oleksak –*
> *Founders of Bantam Bagels*

Chapter 12

IT'S ABOUT GIVE AND TAKE

No matter how brilliant your mind or strategy, if you're playing a solo game, you'll always lose out to a team.

Reid Hoffman – LinkedIn co-founder

We've seen how **Initiative** helps provide us with the inner force that drives us to tackle a task on our own. This characteristic is what sets wheels in motion and sees ideas through to completion regardless if assistance is lacking. It takes challenges as they come and figures out ways to overcome them, or finds another way to get around the roadblock.

Initiative is an important existing element in both the self-starter and the effective leader. If you want to be a success and stand out from the fucking crowd, then you need to take a different path or perform a different approach than everyone else.

That, in essence, is true leadership. Like Jim Schroer, Principal of The New England Consulting Group, Inc., told me during our interview:

Most people take the paved road. On the other hand, there's a certain kind of person that just can't do that and I'd be one of those. I have

> always said, "Take the road not taken". The brambles and the bushes and the pitfalls and the crevices, corners and dark things you didn't know were going to be there... it is just more interesting to take the road of new ventures.
>
> If you want to be a changer, if you want to be a leader, you're better off in situations where the changes are actually required.

However, "going it alone" is not always a smart or effective strategy. Even though you may have strong **Initiative** at the beginning of your endeavors that drives you to take the steps toward success, it is certain that you will require assistance along the way in order to realize your goals.

Take, for example, youth. Babies have a natural desire to explore the world. However, they require adults to help them learn to feed and dress themselves, walk without assistance and venture into the world on their own.

Even though kids have an inner drive to "go it alone", they require help getting on their feet and figuring certain aspects of life out. A child left on their own without any help would be at a great disadvantage and stunted in their abilities, if they survived at all, over a child who had such assistance.

When I was conducting my interview with Dr. Cindy Trimm, we touched on this topic. She said:

> If you look at a child as they're growing, they get to the point where they start wanting to do things themselves,

> where they have a sense of self-direction and they have a sense of internal drive to want to become better. You see it with a child learning how to walk, being weaned from a bottle and learning how to talk. I think it's in each one of us. That seed of greatness is there.
>
> I think that we never lost touch with that and we have the audacity to believe we can make a difference, and we go ahead and do it. We believe we can be successful and we go ahead and do it. We don't ask permission.

At every stage of our journey, we have people that help us along the way.

Of course, when we are young, we have more authorities who influence us than when we grow older, but authoritative guidance remains with us throughout life.

We start out with parents and then move to school where teachers guide us. School gives us access to books that provide us with various bits of insight, perspective, thought and instruction.

We have government, police, religious institutions and other social authorities that offer their influence and then we move to different areas such as military or civilian jobs where further influence is offered and sometimes even forced upon us.

All of these sources shape our personalities and develop our characteristics. Some people are happy living under the influence of others and some people, who have **Initiative**, come to a point where they say "I would prefer to fucking do it myself!"

The Wisdom of Accepting Help

Strength is multiplied through numbers and relying on the help of your teammates and partners (as discussed in chapter 10) is often critical to the overall success of your mission. Like in the opening quote of this chapter says, you can't beat a team if you're a lone player. Earl Monroe illustrated earlier how a single player without **Initiative** on a team can cause that team to sacrifice momentum and lose the game.

Initiative is the ability to strike out on your own. But it also consists of the ability to best assess a situation and take a helping hand when you fucking need it.

I am where I am today because I have partnered with great mentors, business associates, friends and employees throughout my journey who have provided assistance, support and encouragement along the way.

I'm here to tell you that I've accomplished what I have in life because I've got G.R.I.T. Sure, I have had to take the **Initiative** to do a majority of the work on my own. However, I am also proud to admit that I've had some amazing help from individuals that got me through some really nasty shit and dark times.

What you have to do is to ensure that the people you bring into your life and invite to walk with you towards your goals are not fucking chicken-shits and idiots!

You want to surround yourself with people that have the same mindset as you and that have qualities that enhance your own.

You want people surrounding you that have G.R.I.T.!

A good example of this was provided by Sheri Riley who is an empowerment speaker, life strategist and author. Sheri told me:

> I'm a woman of faith, the Word of God, prayer and really believing the Word of God has been everything. When I couldn't see clearly, I believed the Word.
>
> But in addition to my faith, I've had a really good network of people that when I was on laying on the floor crying, both literally and figuratively, and could not get myself up, I could dial the numbers on my phone and call a friend. They helped me. They talked to me. They reassured me.
>
> Having a network of people who know how to help you get up when you can't get up yourself is very important. Even the most driven person, even the most confident person, sometimes has moments when they need someone to pick them up.

You can also take the following analogy as an example of what I'm talking about. One cord will break under a relatively small amount of pressure. However, you wrap four, five, six, or more together then you have a rope that can withstand a hell of a lot of force.

Of course, the stronger the cords you chose to put together, the stronger your combined effort will be against bigger forces and the greater your chances of achieving even greater success.

When it comes time to take the **Initiative** to put together teams and partnerships, choose winners!

Being a Source of Strength

As you take advantage of the help you're given and glean the lessons of life that have come from your attempts and failures, you will eventually come to a place where you are not only more independent, but you become the helping force to someone else.

This is one of the great rewards of having the **Initiative** to achieve your goals.

Of course, you are going out there, picking up the torch and fighting battles for yourself. But you are also pressing through the struggles so that your family, your friends, your partners and others less privileged than you can benefit from your contribution to the world... your success.

Slaying the dragon is a personal achievement that feels really good. But dragging that bastard back to the tribe and experiencing the feeling of sharing your accomplishment with them is the icing on the cake!

I've had the privilege of reaching that point in a major way and I can tell you, it feels fucking incredible!

But first, it's time for you to show some **Initiative** and get to the bottom of all of this by turning the page.

Tenacity is the glue that holds together everything we've discussed so far.

TWO CENTS' WORTH

I believe in a "do as I do, not as I say" culture. If you are perceived as taking the initiative and doing things honestly, employees are empowered to do the same.

If employees see you hammering someone for making a mistake, they will take far fewer risks.

However, if they see you finding teachable moments when things don't go quite right, they will be more comfortable coloring outside the lines.

– John Katzman – Founder of The Princeton Review and Founder and CEO of Noodle

05

T is for Tenacity

Chapter 13

THE FOUR TRAITS OF TENACITY

Patience and tenacity are worth more than twice their weight in cleverness.

Thomas Huxley – English biologist

These words were offered by biologist Thomas Huxley who was referred to as "Darwin's Bulldog" because he held onto Darwin's theory of evolution and refused to let go.

"Darwinism" replaced the more extreme religious view of "creationism" as the mainstream scientific source of humanity largely through Huxley's tenacious efforts.

Bulldog is an appropriate representation of this characteristic of G.R.I.T.

These canines were bred to do battle. Several animals were tethered to a bull (and later bears) and wagers were made on which dog would grab the son-of-a-bitch by the snout, bring it down and pin it to the ground.

It takes a hell of a lot of **Tenacity** to drop an opponent that is many times bigger and stronger than you!

Yet these dogs, with their stout bodies, muscular frames, wide jaws and tenacious attitudes would do just that, even though many faced injury and death in the sport. These dogs bite down and don't let go until the victory has been won!

That is exactly what you have to do with your visions, your dreams and your goals. You have to get a bite on them and refuse to let go regardless.

Huxley was a labeled a "bulldog" because he faced the overwhelming odds of convincing his peers of a theory that was not only new, but went against the grain of their present day system.

Did Huxley devise clever ways to make the Theory of Evolution acceptable?

No! Like a bulldog, he resorted to patience and **Tenacity** to wear his opponents down. He researched, presented the work and waited for the words to sink in, and then researched, presented and waited some more until he wore the assholes out!

Then, like a bulldog, Huxley grabbed the challenge by the snout in its moment of doubt and weakness and pulled the son-of-a-bitch down. It may have been Darwin that came up with the original idea, but it was Huxley's **Tenacity** that forever changed how the world looks at the source of things.

NOTE

Tenacity gives you the ability to become and be whoever you want to be or to do whatever you want to do because you don't see your competition as competition. You don't see the obstacles before you as obstacles.

You're just abiding in the energy of being what you are becoming. There are always going to be obstacles, but the only way obstacles get in your way is if you give them relevance.

– Bill Duke – Actor, Director, Producer, Writer, Humanitarian and Founder of Duke Media Entertainment

Let's take a look at the components of this bulldog-like characteristic.

Trait One: *Perseverance*

Perseverance is defined as the ability to hold fast to a task despite any difficulty or delay encountered towards achieving success. This is the trait of **Tenacity** that grabs hold of the dream and doesn't fucking let go!

Dale Carnegie, the famous writer, lecturer and self-improvement specialist, said:

"Most of the important things in the world have been accomplished by people who have kept on trying when there seemed to be no hope at all."

That, my friends, is perseverance and the foundational essence of **Tenacity**. You continue on through the darkness, through the storms, through the resistance, through whatever fucking obstacle gets in your way... even when there appears to be no ray of hope... until you reach your goal.

If you're going to succeed, you have to possess the **Tenacity** to fucking persevere!

Trait Two: *Passion*

The depth of **Tenacity** needed to get through the darkest, nastiest and most hopeless times doesn't exist without passion.

Perseverance may be the essence of **Tenacity**, but passion gives this trait a stronger and more solid staying power.

Passion is an emotion, but it's much more than that. Merriam-Webster defines passion as "a strong feeling of enthusiasm or excitement for something or about doing something."

When you're up against mountainous obstacles in life, it can be extremely difficult to muster up anything but fear, doubt and depression, much less feel enthusiasm and excitement. But that is exactly what **Tenacity** is all about.

When the struggle is the darkest and most hopeless, you've got to dig down and continue fighting with enthusiasm and excitement... with passion... for your dream!

It is tenacious passion that gives you that extra push, extra drive and extra strength to overcome and reach the summit of that mother-fucking mountain.

TWO CENTS' WORTH

> Finding that thing that you're passionate about is the key. Once you do that, the rest of it, even though it's still hard, becomes easier because you've got that passion and that fire behind what you're doing and what you're facing.
>
> *– Suzanne Smith – Founder of Social Impact Architects*

Trait Three: *Faith*

The ability to hang on until the fucking end requires another trait... faith.

You have to have such a strong faith that nothing can cast a shadow so dark that it snuffs out your light.

Now, some people choose to place their faith in an outside source, like a deity, spirit, or some established man-made process. That's all well and good, but what I'm talking about is a belief in yourself and in your dream that is so deep and so strong that nothing stops you from accomplishing your desires.

When the entire fucking world tells you that it cannot be done, you have to be able to shout right back at them that YES IT CAN!

This type of faith has caused thousands upon thousands of souls to make it through their darkest valleys and come out on the other side to claim victory.

A lack of faith, in yourself and in your dreams, is a weak link in your **Tenacity**.

When you are beaten down, exhausted and feeling the pain of defeat, faith is often the element that provides a lifeline out of the pit of defeat, placing your feet back onto the road to success.

Trait Four: *Flexibility*

Flexibility may seem like an odd trait to be associated with bulldog-like **Tenacity**.

However, it is actually one of the foundational pillars of this part of G.R.I.T. When you're flexible, you have the capability of easily bending and conforming to various pressures, whether expected or unexpected.

Having flexibility means you are both willing and able to change or try new approaches.

Although **Tenacity** means you bite into your vision or goal and clamp down on it with a locked jaw, it also includes being flexible enough to bend, conform and change when life is tossing you around like a fucking Rag Doll.

I learned early in life that I had to be flexible as well as tenacious while pursuing my career path that led from one job to another. If one company or position wasn't fulfilling my drive, or I outgrew where I was at, then I needed to be flexible enough to move onward in pursuit of my ultimate goal.

Even fighters are taught to be flexible. A rigid stance may look intimidating, but it is the flexibility of bending with the punches, conforming to your opponents moves and changing with the turn of events that makes you a winner.

Sometimes, you need to stand strong like the mighty oak against the raging storms and, sometimes, it's best to bend with the winds like the poplar.

If you're not flexible when the need arises, you could snap and break.

When you're hanging onto your dream with all you've got, don't fail to be flexible enough to give your **Tenacity** greater power!

Chapter 14

HOW TO BE THE LAST ONE STANDING

Diamonds are nothing more than chunks of coal that stuck to their jobs.

Malcolm Forbes - American entrepreneur

The junkyard of life is piled high with failed dreams and ideas. Surprisingly, the majority of these are not due to anything other than their owners giving up on them before they came to desired fruition.

There simply wasn't enough fucking **Tenacity** to see those projects through.

This trait called **Tenacity** is the quantifier of the change, the action and that part of you that can, as Kipling put it:

"Force your heart and nerve and sinew to serve your turn long after they are gone."

It is that grab-ahold-and-don't-let-go attitude that has seen a host of people through their darkest tunnels, bringing them into the shining light of success at the other end.

The world as we know it would be considerably different if it wasn't for the deep down, gut-anchored courage we call **Tenacity**.

TRUISM

> Success is no accident. It is hard work, perseverance, learning, studying, sacrifice and, most of all, love of what you are doing or learning to do.
>
> ***– Pelé – Soccer Great***

There are hundreds of examples of people who have been beaten down, often more than once, but have refused to quit and hung on until success was reached.

A few examples of these outstanding folks are:

- Thomas Edison – As an impressionable student, Edison was told by his teachers that he was "too stupid to learn anything." After school, he ended up being fired from his first two jobs because he wasn't productive enough. Edison had all the reasons in the world to say "fuck it!" and settle for mediocrity, but he didn't quit. His **Tenacity** led him to become one of the most life-changing inventors in modern history with over 1,000 patents.

- Henry Ford – When first starting out, Henry failed miserably at his first couple of automobile businesses and sullied his reputation. He didn't let that stop him though. He presented his assembly line ideas to various people before finally finding a partner that would back him. The rest, as they say, is history.

- Pelé (Edson Arantes do Nascimento) – Considered by many to be the greatest soccer player ever, Pelé faced massive challenges from the start. He grew up in extremely poor conditions in Sao Paulo, Brazil where he practiced his passion using a stuffed sock or grapefruit and raised money to chase his dream by working as a servant. However, Pelé himself credits his harsh beginnings with giving him the **Tenacity** to overcome rivals and challenges of the game.

- Oprah Winfrey – Oprah always wanted to be on television and share her passion for news and real-life stories. She overcame obstacles early on by becoming both the youngest female and first black female news anchor at a Nashville television station. However, when she moved on to a Baltimore station, she was deemed "too emotionally invested in her stories". Funny thing, Oprah took that passion and emotion for sharing life stories and turned it into a $3 billion media empire where she wears the title of "Queen of All Media".

- Jim Abbott – Born without a right hand, Jim Abbott could have been prevented from playing sports from the start

However, Jim had **Tenacity** and he refused to listen to all the naysayers that told him he "can't".

- Jim was an effective quarterback and pitcher in his Michigan high school and went on to lead the University of Michigan to two Big Ten championships, assisted the U.S.A. to place second at the 1987 Pan American Games, pitched in the final game of the 1988 Summer Olympics to help the U.S. team win an unofficial gold medal and was picked up by the California Angels in 1988 as their eighth choice. He was the first baseball player to win the James E. Sullivan Award for top amateur athlete, became the 1988 Big Ten Athlete of the Year and was elected to the College Baseball Hall of Fame in 2007. Abbott achieved all of that with only one fucking hand!

There are many other examples of people that have been ridiculed and rejected only to bite into their dreams and hold on until they produced success. This type of courage is what keeps our faith intact as we are submitted to the refining fires of rejection, belittling, discouragement and other harsh trials.

NOTE

There are many stories that I think we've all grown up with. The one that often comes to my mind is Thomas Edison talking about how many failures it took to invent the light bulb.

> And then there are sayings like the difference between the successful person and the failure is the successful person has failed more often.
>
> *– John McNeil – President and CEO of Cancer Treatment Centers of America*

Tenacity Means Hard Work

One of the defining qualities of **Tenacity** is putting in a lot of hard, often grueling, work towards the goals you have chosen to pursue.

Successful people don't fit into such mediocre molds. Goals are always kept in sight and milestones have to be met along the way. Making your dreams come true just doesn't happen if you're not willing to burn the midnight oil, work a lot of weekends and push, push, push!

I sat down with co-founder of Sports195, Aaron Earls, who is also communications, marketing and sales executive and successful entrepreneur.

Aaron, like me, enjoys surrounding himself with inspiring quotes of successful people. During our discussion about **Tenacity**, he started off with a Mohammad Ali quote and expanded on it. He shared it this way:

> Muhammad Ali said, "The fight is won or lost far away from witnesses, behind the lines, in the gym and out there on the road, long before I dance under those lights."
>
> I think it's really symbolic that, in order to achieve the equivalent of "dancing under those lights" – whatever profession you're in – you've got to put in the work. Putting in the work is getting up early, working late potentially and also working smartly, but working incredibly hard.
>
> Whether you're a boxer and you're jumping rope or pounding the bag to the equivalent of that in a corporate environment, that level of tenacity is critical to everybody's success.

If you want to win the victory and achieve your goals, you have to be ready, willing and able to dig in and work to get there. A great deal of that work is the day-in, day-out drudgery that the masses who are admiring your success never see or know about.

Success is definitely not for the fucking lazy!

TRUISM

> I don't know how I built tenacity. I'd like to say that it came from my parents, but talking with them about my three-year-old self, I feel like it was just always there.
>
> *– Abby Jordan – Co-Founder of eCreamy Ice Cream and Gelato Gifts*

Overcoming overwhelming grief and challenges through tenacious G.R.I.T. is something Linda Losey, entrepreneur, author, artist and founder of Bloomery Plantation Distillery, knows about on a very personal level.

During our interview, Linda shared the following:

> Losing two sons, through two separate tragedies, thrust me into a sphere of despair that I hope no parent ever has to face. I was pushed to the edge and emerged with wisdom, compassion and grace... and, oh yes, tenacity!
>
> I had to rise above. Rise above the ashes that became my grief. I shouted out to God, to the Universe, to whomever or whatever was out there and I found my grit, my courage and my reason for being.
>
> For all those who want to build tenacity, I urge you to step out of your comfort zone now. However, push through by your own choosing. Don't wait to be blindsided by a crushing blow that, by its very nature, will help build the core of who you are.
>
> I've given up, but never quit.
>
> I've moved forward by taking action and growing.
>
> Every second. Every minute. Every hour. Every day.
>
> Little by little, with every step, progress was made.

And when I look over my shoulder and see all I endured,

I shake my head in disbelief.

"Jeez, how did I get through that? How did I?"

It still amazes me.

In order to be a champion like Muhammad Ali, Linda Losey or any of the other examples offering their words of wisdom in this book, you have to, day after fucking day, get up early, punch, run, sweat, stay up late, and work your ass off. Victory and success come, but they come at a price.

If you think that reaching your goals requires anything less than you may have the wrong mindset.

The Winner Mindset

Tenacity has its base in a certain way of thinking... a way of thinking that only winners know and understand.

Every single person that can be labeled as "successful" has this mindset.

If you have or are willing to develop this same way of thinking, then you too can be successful in any arena you choose.

What am I talking about? You have to love what you're doing and you have to enjoy the journey even when the road gets fucking tough. A lot of people start out believing that success is all about how much money you can make, but that thinking is all wrong.

Although the money is definitely nice and allows you to enjoy a lot of things that you normally couldn't afford, the bottom line is that you have to love what you're doing especially since you'll spend a tremendous amount of time actually doing it. Because time can't be bought.

Travis Steffen is the founder of 7 companies and co-founder of several others so he knows about **Tenacity** and how to become a success. Travis told me during our interview that:

> At the end of the day, you have to be doing what you're doing for the right reasons, because you love the journey. It's because you enjoy making progress. You enjoy solving problems, satisfying your customers, leaving your legacy.
>
> If you're interested in the money only, go work on Wall Street. That's where the money's at if you just want a quick buck. But at the same time, what are you really doing with your life? If you care about that answer, then I think tenacity is probably one of the more important things you can have.
>
> But just like all these things, it's different for everyone so you kind of have to find out what it is you want to apply that kind of mindset to and be honest with yourself.

Just as Travis pointed out, and like practically every successful person that lives will emphasize, being a success is almost 100 percent up to you. If you want to succeed, then you will apply the G.R.I.T. necessary to get started, overcome the obstacles and setbacks, and fucking see it through to the end.

That's how it's done... that's how the successful people do it and that's how you can do it too. But it's up to you and you alone to make the determination to be a success. No one, and I fucking mean no one, can do that for you!

The Takeaway

Do you have the fucking **Tenacity** to start and see one, two, a dozen or more businesses fail before striking your goal? Not many people do.

There isn't anything special about successful people except they have a winner's attitude... they've got G.R.I.T.

Thomas Jefferson once said:

"Nothing can stop the man with the right mental attitude from achieving his goal; nothing on earth can help the man with the wrong mental attitude."

If you're not willing to pay the price at the beginning, or if you give up and throw in the towel at any point along the way, you will not reach your goal... you will not be a success.

And like Tom so eloquently stated... there's nothing on the face of this planet that can help you. Not me or anyone or anything else will make a difference because you have set your mind to fail.

However, if you do have the mindset of a winner then it won't matter how many times you fall down and fail. You'll get your ass up and rise like the fucking Phoenix until you embrace your dreams and desires.

Then you hold onto those fuckers with the **Tenacity** of a bulldog until they are realities!

Chapter 15

THRIVING, NOT SURVIVING

I thrive on obstacles. If I'm told that it can't be told, then I push harder.

Issa Rae – actress, writer, director

The desire to survive is one of the strongest in the human psyche. People will take all sorts of actions, both good and bad, to ensure their survival.

If you are facing starvation, an attack by an enemy, or some horrible natural calamity then you want to take full advantage of your survival instincts. That shit will get you through times that are trying to kill you!

However, this is a book about success... in business and in life.

The problem with a lot of people is they have misplaced survival instincts. They let their desire to survive overcome their desire to succeed in both of these areas.

And the thing about survival instincts is that they will cause you to NOT take any fucking risks!

As we've clearly seen, achieving your goals and being a success involves taking risks and then holding on to your dreams like a ravenous bulldog until they manifest.

Being a success and thriving in life is the opposite of surviving!

NOTE

Tenacity is a wily duck-and-dive approach to always quietly having a plan B when plan A goes perhaps slightly awry.

– Lara Morgan - Entrepreneur and Founder of CompanyShortcuts.com

If you want to survive, go to your shitty job and draw your pathetic paycheck. It will give you enough to put food in your mouth, clothes on your back and a roof over your head.

After all that survival shit is taken care of, you might... MIGHT have enough left over to live a little. With the middle class crashing in this country, that gets more difficult to do with each passing day. If you continue in that survivalist mindset, you just may be practicing REAL survival one day soon.

However, if you want to thrive... if you want to enjoy some really nice shit in life and go to some really exotic places... if you want to have enough to not have to worry about financial woes... if you want to have extra to give to relatives, friends and the less fortunate... then you need to throw that survivalist attitude the fuck out with yesterday's garbage and get out there and practice some **Tenacity**!

What people don't fucking understand is that when they choose to be mediocre and go to the 9 to 5 job that they can't fucking stand, they are actually practicing **Tenacity**, only in a negative, survivalist sense.

They are being tenacious about living a mediocre life. When thoughts of grandeur arise about fulfilling their dreams, they tenaciously knock those fuckers down and say, "No! I will NOT risk fulfilling my dreams. I choose instead to sit here in my safe fucking comfy spot. I will SURVIVE, damn it!"

Hey, if that's you then I don't fucking know why you're reading this book. Obviously, you have chosen to sit safely on your ass, take very little risk and survive. You may live a long fucking life and make it to a ripe-old age, but I can guarantee that you will not have truly lived and you definitely will not have thrived.

On the other hand, if you are in this situation I'm describing and you have read this book to this point then maybe, just maybe, you want to throw off the chains of mediocrity, say "fuck it!" to surviving and get out there and make your dreams come true.

If that's the case, bite into that bitch with **Tenacity** and don't let go until your goals have been met, your dreams are fulfilled and your life is thriving.

NOTE

I define tenacity by saying, "It's how many times we decided to get up". It's easy to quit, stop and give up.

That's why I choose tenacity all day long! It's what gets you through the tough times. I meet so many book smart people that can't handle a rough day let along a rough year.

– Clarence Bethea – Founder and CEO of Upsie

Do You Want to Flourish or Flounder?

To thrive means to prosper and flourish, which is a far cry from sitting on your ass and surviving.

I've heard thousands of people throughout my journey scream things like I can't succeed because... I don't have the time! I don't have the money! I don't have the education! I don't have the connections! I grew up in the wrong neighborhood! I've been mistreated! Blah! Blah! Fucking blah!

Every single one of those excuses and any like them are coming from a survivalist, "poor me" mentality. Those types of negative thoughts will only leave you floundering and flopping like a fucking fish on dry land.

With such an attitude, you will be mediocre and miserable your entire life. And you know what? It isn't the fault of any of these outside sources... it's fucking YOUR fault!

I don't give a shit what your background is. If you have **Tenacity,** then you will find a way to make your dreams come true despite ANY obstacles that you may THINK are standing in the way. Because, you see, all those towering dark and evil demons are in your fucking head!

It's a fact... when you step out of your comfortable life of survival, you will come upon a lot of scary shit that will attempt to send you scurrying back to your dark, dingy and mediocre safe-hole.

But if you get out there and stay out there, you will fight, you will fail and, sometimes, you will win. It's all part of the spiraling pathway that leads to success.

But if you want to thrive in life then you will have to take those steps, fight those battles, embrace the failures and get back up and do it again until you win!

TWO CENTS' WORTH

Tenacity is having the will to *THRIVE* in spite of life's lickings. A will that's powered by hope and perseverance towards attaining more than what was envisioned to be so you can live, truly live!

– Linda Losey - Entrepreneur, Owner of Bloomery Plantation Distillery, Best-selling Author & Award-winning Artist

What a lot of people tend to do in order to justify not taking the risks towards manifesting their goals is to convince themselves to "wait on the right opportunity."

Well, guess what? Those golden opportunities seldom, if ever, drop out of the fucking sky and land in your lap. Ninety-nine percent of those opportunities are made... by getting out there, working hard and tenaciously holding on until what you're doing finally spits out what you want.

TRUISM

I built tenacity to be successful by being willing to be audacious which includes three very specific things.

One is my uncompromising unwillingness to sacrifice my thrill of living for anybody or anything, whether it's people, money, influence, or whatever it happens to be. I will not sacrifice my thrill of living.

The second is that I will only pursue my calling. In business, that means I only work with people who authentically want what I most love to offer.

The third is teachability. I'm constantly growing, learning and expanding because the day I stop doing that, I die.

– Dr. David Gruder – Business Peak Performance Psychologist, Macro Strategist and Cultural Architect

The Takeaway

You may be as content and happy as a pig in shit sitting and surviving in your comfort zone.

Whether you flourish and thrive in life, or whether you flounder like a fish trying to survive, both choices are in your control.

I'm here to tell you that if you want more out of life... if you want to fucking prosper then you need to apply some **Tenacity** and the other elements of G.R.I.T. and go forth and conquer!

The question is... do you have the G.R.I.T. to take the steps, weather the storms, learn the lessons and, by God, grab a hold until you reach your destination?

If so then it's totally up to you to go after and achieve what you want out of life. The decision and ability are both in your hands.

You simply need to embrace and apply G.R.I.T.

Conclusion

NOW IT'S YOUR TURN - IMPROVISE, ADAPT AND OVERCOME

Setting a goal is not the main thing. It is deciding how you will go about achieving it and staying with that plan.

Tom Landry – American football player, coach

There's a saying that is widely used in the Marine Corps which says:

"Improvise, adapt and overcome!"

That, in a nutshell, is what my G.R.I.T. mindset is all about.

You've got to have the **Guts** to step out of your comfort zone and face the fears of failure.

You've got to have the **Resilience** to weather the storms and get back up when you get the shit kicked out of you.

You've got to have the **Initiative** to press forward on your own when help isn't around.

And you've got to have the **Tenacity** to stick with the pursuit of your dream and your goals in spite of all the bullshit you encounter along the way.

Of course, the first step is to have a goal, but as long time Dallas Cowboys coach, Tom Landry, pointed out in the opening quote, it is the plan to fulfill that goal and then sticking to it that is the most important aspect.

The world is full of people who have goals, but those that actually take the steps and do the things necessary to bring them to fulfillment are few and far between.

The ones who reach their goals and make their dreams come true are the ones who focus on what they want and then march headlong toward it. If they get knocked down and fail, they get the fuck back up and keep right on marching.

Successful people don't give up and they don't take "no" for an answer.

They have G.R.I.T.

Coming Full Circle

So, at this point, you might be asking, "Is it really worth taking the risks, paying the price and facing a constant stream of resistance to attain your goals?"

It most certainly is and I'll tell you why.

G.R.I.T. has got me through some very dark and tough times. I have gone through the extreme rigors of the Marine Corps while injured, lost good jobs on numerous occasions, battled cancer and now continue to deal with the horrible fucking side effects of it, created companies without a formal education, and bounced back from a divorce, etc., etc.

Instead of letting those events in life grind me down into the dirt and accepting a "poor me" defeatist attitude. I got back the fuck up and overcame each hurdle until I became the success I am today.

I didn't simply overcome these challenges. I fucking tackled them and did something about them.

When I was told I couldn't have a successful company because I didn't have a fucking college education, I went out and built a highly successful one anyway.

My company, AKQURACY, has been chosen for Inc. Magazine's *List of Fastest Growing Private Companies*. On top of that, I was selected to join the Young Entrepreneur Council (YEC) that is comprised of the world's most successful young entrepreneurs, and I have been a semi-finalist for Entrepreneur Magazine's

Entrepreneur of the Year award, among various other achievements, awards and acknowledgements.

When I was diagnosed with testicular cancer, became infertile, lost my fucking hormones and experienced muscular degeneration, I didn't cry about it.

No. I funded my own fucking research so that I could save myself and so that others who walk in my footsteps face less of a burden

Listen, going through the horrors of cancer and becoming a cancer survivor was not on my fucking bucket list!

However, with equal enthusiasm, I can tell you that it was one of the best things to happen to me in my life. It enhanced my perspective, strengthened my G.R.I.T. and taught me to truly care about others.

One of the biggest lessons I learned from having cancer was that you cannot look at someone and know what they have been through or what their present challenges are.

The point of sharing this is that I have faced major obstacles in life, some of which would have made a lot of people lie down and give the fuck up, only to get my ass back up and overcome. The G.R.I.T. that I have and that I have developed over my life has led me to a place of thriving success where I not only can enjoy the good things of life myself, but I can share my excess with others.

BOTH of those factors make the process well worth the effort.

The Rest of Your Life Starts Today

It doesn't matter where you are today. You may be just starting out on your journey, you may be cowering in some dark corner after being scared by some horrible shit that has happened in your life, or you may be starting to understand that you need to develop a bit more character to push you over the hill to your goal.

Hell, you may even feel you're at the age where it's too late to start. It really doesn't matter where you're at in life. The bottom line is that you need to enjoy the fucking journey while making positive things happen. If you go at it with that attitude, you'll not only make pleasing accomplishments, but you'll have one hell of a good time in the process, both of which improve the quality of life all around.

Like I mentioned earlier, success can be fucking addicting! Most successful people could easily retire early and just sit back and enjoy the fruits of their labor. But the thing is... we enjoy the process of G.R.I.T.!

Regardless of where you're at along life's journey, the rest of your life starts TODAY! Right fucking NOW!

There are absolutely no excuses.

TRUISM

> You know, I would suspect that someone who is reading about this is someone who probably already has G.R.I.T. I think it starts with determination.
>
> I would suspect that the reader of a book on guts, resilience, initiative and tenacity is somebody who is making it their life's quest to have those things.
>
> And how do you become a better leader? By studying leaders and by looking at every opportunity of how you can learn to be a better leader yourself.
>
> ***– John McNeil – President and CEO of Cancer Treatment Centers of America***

All you need to do is follow the advice in this book, develop some fucking G.R.I.T. and go out there and take what you want.

Sure, it's going to take a lot of work and you're going to have times where you want to give up. But you have to have the **Guts** to get out there, the **Resilience** to keep fucking marching forward, the **Initiative** to keep things moving alone if need be, and the **Tenacity** to chase your dreams and not let go until they have been fulfilled.

You have to see each failure as a success because it teaches you lessons. Then take that knowledge and experience and improvise, adapt and overcome!

Keep pushing, keep fighting and keep working.

And remember... **No one EVER drowned in sweat!**

Index of Contributors

The following are the contributors of quotes, opinions, and other words of wisdom to this book and appear in the approximate order of appearance.

Daniel Day-Lewis – English actor

Sgt. Maj. William H. Bly, Jr. – Marine Corps – Retired

September Dohrmann – COO of CEO Space International

Crystal Paine – founder of MoneySavingMom.com

Wayne Gretzky – former Canadian NHL hockey player and head coach

Wade Davis – Canadian scientist, author and photographer

Linda Losey – entrepreneur, owner of Bloomery Plantation Distillery, author and artist

Brenda Coffman – founder and CEO of Blondie's Cookies, Inc.

Neale Donald Walsch – American author, actor, screenwriter and speaker

Jim Rohn – American entrepreneur, author and motivational speaker

Rick Hinnant – entrepreneur and co-founder (with wife Melissa) of Grace & Lace

Andy Paige – beauty and style expert, TV personality, entrepreneur and author of Style on a Shoestring

Rebecca Rescate – founder of CitiKitty and Rebecca Rescate Inc. and co-founder of HoodiePillow

Ines Temple – president of LHH-DBM Peru and LHH Chile, president of CARE Peru and author of Usted S.A. Empleabilidad y Marketing Personal

Randi Ilyse Roth – lawyer and founding member of the Academy of Court-Appointed Masters (ACAM). Primary author of the original 2006 version of the ACAM bench book entitled Appointing Special Masters and Other Judicial Adjuncts: A Handbook for Judges.

Andy Thompson – pastor of World Overcomers Christian Church

Fleetwood Hicks –founder and president of Villy Custom

Michelle Patterson – president of Global Women Foundation and founder, president and CEO of Women Network LLC

Scot Anderson – Christian comedian, motivational speaker and executive coach

Kim Nelson – founder of Daisy Cakes

Halle Berry – model, actress and producer

Omar Tyree – author, novelist and entrepreneur

Paul LeJoy – author, entrepreneur and owner of Pacific Realty Partners

Jonathan Bender – NBA basketball player, entrepreneur and inventor

Dan Rothwell – entrepreneur and electrical engineer

Winston Churchill – former British Prime Minister, statesman and writer

Franklin D. Roosevelt – former U.S. President (32nd), statesman and political leader

John Frederick (Jay) Jones – attorney, entrepreneur and owner of Jones Scones

Nick and Elyse Oleksak – founders and owners of Bantam Bagels

Dr. Kevin Kruger – President of NASPA - Student Administrators in Higher Education

Franklin P. Jones – reporter, public relations executive and humorist

Ann Landers – Dear Abby syndicated columnist (Note: Ann Landers was a pen name for Ruth Crowley from 1943 to 1955 and then Esther Pauline "Eppie" Lederer from 1955 to 2002)

Li Gang – CEO of DloDlo

Suzanne Smith – founder of Social Impact Architects

Bonnie Kanner – founder of Shooting Star Entertainment

Tiffany Krumins – entrepreneur, inventor and creator of Ava the Elephant® talking medicine dispensers for children

Roxi Bahar Hewertson – CEO of Highland Consulting Group

John Dewey – American psychologist, educational reformer and philosopher

Dan Caldwell – entrepreneur and co-founder of TapouT

Billy Mann – former CEO and president of New Music A&R and president of Global Artist Management for EMI

Chester Elton – author, executive consultant, motivational speaker, trainer, employee engagement expert and founder and CEO of The Culture Works

Marc Williams – founder and CEO of Williams Communications

Bev Vines-Haines and Charlotte Clary – founders and owners of Ice Chips

Dr. David Gruder – business peak performance psychologist, macro strategist and cultural architect

Stacey Ferreira – entrepreneur, speaker, author and co-founder of MySocialCloud and co-founder and CEO of Forrge

Zig Ziglar – salesman, author and motivational speaker

Lara Morgan – entrepreneur and founder of CompanyShortcuts.com

Dr. Harold Koenig – physician, author and director of the Center for Spirituality, Theology and Health at Duke University Medical Center

Robert "Bo" Bennett – American businessman

Jim Schroer – marketing innovator and principal of The New England Consulting Group, Inc.

Stephen Richards – author and investigative journalist

Scott Gerber – founder of the Young Entrepreneur Council (YEC), public speaker, international business columnist and author of Never Get a "Real" Job: How to Dump Your Boss, Build a Business and Not Go Broke

R. Scott Arnell – founding partner of Geneva Capital

Earl Monroe – basketball player for the Baltimore Bullets and New York Knicks

Dr. Cindy Trimm – author, empowerment specialist and high-impact teacher

Jonny Imerman – founder of Imerman Angels

Reid Hoffman – founder of LinkedIn

Sheri Riley – certified personal development and leadership coach, life strategist and empowerment speaker

John Katzman – founder of The Princeton Review, founder and CEO of Noodle

Thomas Huxley – English biologist

Bill Duke – actor, director, producer, writer, humanitarian and founder of Duke Media Entertainment

Dale Carnegie – writer, lecturer and self-improvement specialist

Malcolm Forbes – American entrepreneur

Joseph Rudyard Kipling – English journalist, writer, poet and novelist

Pelé (Edson Arantes do Nascimento) – Brazilian soccer player

John McNeil – president and CEO of Cancer Treatment Centers of America

Aaron Earls – entrepreneur, co-founder of Sports195 and communications, marketing and sales executive

Abby Jordan – co-founder of eCreamy Ice Cream and Gelato Gifts

Travis Steffen – entrepreneur, founder and co-founder of numerous companies

Thomas Jefferson – former U.S. President, Vice President, statesman and principle author of the Declaration of Independence

Issa Rae – actress, writer and director

Clarence Bethea – founder and CEO of Upsie

Tom Landry – American football player and coach

About the Author

Scott Petinga has risen through such oppositions as failure, rejection, divorce and even cancer to accomplish impressive and respectable goals and now has this insatiable drive, this compulsion to create change. To be change. Everything he pursues must have meaning and purpose beyond the norm.

Petinga is currently the Chief Troublemaker of The Scott Petinga Group where he is a pioneer in the development of businesses that make a lasting impact on society. When he's not busy saving the planet he uses his acquired wisdom, knowledge and experience to help others make their mark in the world.

After serving in the military and in roles as varied as Vice President of Segmentation Management at Santander Bank and Adjunct Professor at several regional colleges, Petinga put his brilliant marketing skills to work. He served in several senior executive roles at advertising agencies, including Accountability Director at Carmichael Lynch and Strategic Planning Director at RMG Connect – JWT, before leaving Madison Avenue in 2007 to launch his flagship company, the data-driven communications agency AKQURACY. Founded on the strength of a single client relationship, Petinga has since grown the company into a multi-million-dollar marketing endeavor.

Within 5 years, AKQURACY earned a spot on Inc. Magazine's prestigious List of Fastest-Growing Private Companies and then

Petinga went on to be selected to join the Young Entrepreneur Council (YEC) – an invite only organization comprised of the world's most successful young entrepreneurs – plus was a semi-finalist for Entrepreneur magazine's "Entrepreneur of the Year" Award.

Petinga is also extremely passionate about serving the community: he is the founder of the TH!NK DIFFERENT Foundation, the Fairy Foundation, the Center of Advocacy for Cancer of the Testes International (CACTI), and a volunteer mentor with Imerman Angels of Chicago.